D1084275

A Day Long To Be Remembered

"The train arrived at Washington at ten minutes to one on Friday morning, and thus ended the dedication of the Gettysburg Cemetery—a day long to be remembered by the Gettysburgers in this to them eventful year, and one whose effects will pass into history."

John Hay, November 21, 1863

This is the last paragraph of an article written by John Hay, President Lincoln's assistant private secretary—published in the Washington <u>Daily Morning Chronicle</u> two days after Lincoln delivered the Gettysburg Address. John Hay was a part-time correspondent for the Washington, D.C. newspaper and joined President Lincoln for the legendary trip.

Lincoln in Gettysburg

Written by Michael Burlingame   Photography by Robert Shaw

Firelight
PUBLISHING
Heyworth, Illinois

In association with John Warner IV

It is fitting that this foundry date appears on the northern end of Cemetery Ridge, directly west of the Lydia Leister farm, General Meade's headquarters during the battle.

. . . It is hard to say that anything has been more bravely, and well done, than at Antietam, Murfreesboro, Gettysburg, and on many fields of lesser note. . . .

LETTER TO JAMES C. CONKLING, SPRINGFIELD, ILLINOIS, AUGUST 26, 1863

. . . And while it has not pleased the Almighty to bless us with a return of peace, we can but press on, guided by the best light He gives us, trusting that in His own good time, and wise way, all will yet be well. . . .

ANNUAL MESSAGE TO CONGRESS, DECEMBER 1, 1862

A REENACTMENT OF THE GIANT BATTLE ON A HOT, HUMID JULY AFTERNOON NEAR THE GETTYSBURG BATTLEFIELD.

Four score and seven yea[rs]

forth, upon this continen[t,]

in liberty, and dedicate[d]

"all men are created eq[ual"]

Now we are engaged in [a]

whether that nation, o[r]

and so dedicated, can [so]

on a great battle field

Washington, ..., 186 .

ago our fathers brought

a new nation, conceived

to the proposition that

al"

a great civil war, testing

any nation so conceived,

long endure. We are met

of that war. We have

Contents

PRECEDING PAGE: THIS QUINTESSENTIAL PORTRAIT OF A DETERMINED, STRONG-WILLED ABRAHAM LINCOLN WAS MADE BY ALEXANDER GARDNER IN WASHINGTON, D.C. ON SUNDAY, NOVEMBER 8, 1863, ELEVEN DAYS BEFORE HE DELIVERED THE GETTYSBURG ADDRESS. DURING THIS PORTRAIT SESSION, GARDNER MADE SEVERAL PHOTOGRAPHS OF LINCOLN, INCLUDING A PORTRAIT OF THE PRESIDENT WITH HIS PERSONAL SECRETARIES JOHN G. NICOLAY AND JOHN HAY. THIS IS A CROPPED IMAGE PROBABLY MADE FROM THE ORIGINAL PLATE OF THE FULL-FRAME PORTRAIT ON PAGE 74. (INDIANA HISTORICAL SOCIETY COLLECTION)

ONE GREAT BATTLE

... in a succession of battles in Pennsylvania, near to us, through three days, so rapidly fought that they might be called one great battle on the 1st, 2d and 3d of the month of July ...

EXTEMPORANEOUS SPEECH AT THE EXECUTIVE MANSION (RESPONSE TO A SERENADE), WASHINGTON, D.C., JULY 7, 1863

In early May 1863, Robert E. Lee's Confederates thrashed the Army of the Potomac under Joseph Hooker at Chancellorsville, Virginia. When a dispatch reporting the outcome of that battle reached the White House, Abraham Lincoln was stunned. With tears streaming down his face, he exclaimed: "My God! my God! What will the country say? What will the country say?" In despair, he sighed: "I am the loneliest man in America."

Shortly after receiving the bad news, Lincoln hastened to the Army of the Potomac and handed Hooker a letter asking: "What next? If possible I would be very glad of another movement early enough to give us some benefit from the fact of the enemies communications being broken, but neither for this reason or any other, do I wish anything done in desperation or rashness. An early movement would also help to supersede the bad moral effect of the recent one, which is sure to be considerably injurious. Have you already in your mind a plan wholly, or partially formed? If you have, prossecute it without interference from me. If you have not, please inform me, so that I, incompetent as I may be, can try [to] assist in the formation of some plan for the Army." Hooker, known as Fighting Joe, said that he planned to remain on the Rappahannock River and strike again when his army was prepared to advance. The visit convinced Lincoln that the army had "suffered no defeat or loss of esprit du corps, but have made a change in the programme (a forced one, to be sure) which promises just as well as did the opening of the campaign."

A week later, Hooker informed the President that he was about to attack Lee, even though he believed that the Confederates had superior numbers. Lincoln demurred, arguing that it "does not now appear probable to me that you can gain anything by an early renewal of the attempt to cross the Rappahannock. I therefore shall not complain, if you do no more, for a time, than to keep the enemy at bay, and out of other mischief, by menaces and occasional cavalry raids, if practicable; and to put your own army in good condition again. Still, if in your own clear judgment, you can renew the attack successfully, I do not mean to restrain you. Bearing upon this last point, I must tell you I have some painful intimations that some of your corps and Division Commanders are not giving you their entire confidence. This would be ruinous, if true; and you should therefore, first of all, ascertain the real facts beyond all possibility of doubt." (Some of Hooker's corps commanders led a revolt against him which fizzled when their choice to head the army— George Gordon Meade of the Fifth Corps—balked.)

Gov. Curtin
Harrisburg, Pa.

EXECUTIVE MANSION,

WASHINGTON, *May 1. 1863.* (10:55 P.M.)

The whole disposable force at Baltimore & elsewhere in reach have already been sent after the enemy which alarms you. The worst thing the enemy could do for himself would be to weaken himself before Hooker, & therefore it is safe to believe he is not doing it; and the best thing he could do for himself, would be to get us so scared as to bring part of Hooker's force away, and that is just what he is trying to do. I will telegraph you in the morning about calling out the militia

A. Lincoln

Telegram to Pennsylvania Governor Andrew Curtain, May 1, 1863

In response to two telegrams from Governor Curtin, received at 4:25 P.M. and 10 P.M., reporting despatches from Pittsburgh and Western Pennsylvania importuning protection against a reported invasion.

Gov. Curtin
Harrisburg, Pa.

EXECUTIVE MANSION,

WASHINGTON, *May 2. 1863.*

Gen. Halleck tells me he has a despatch from Gen. Schenck this morning, informing him that our forces have joined, and that the enemy menacing Penn. will have to fight or run to-day. I hope I am not less anxious to do my duty to Pennsylvania, than yourself; but I really do not yet see the justification for incurring the trouble and expense of calling out the militia. I shall keep watch and try to do my duty.

A. Lincoln

P.S. Our forces are exactly between the enemy and Pennsylvania.

Telegram to Pennsylvania Governor Andrew Curtain, May 2, 1863

General Robert C. Schenck telegraphed from Baltimore, "Railroad clear and working to Grafton. . . . [John R.] Kenly has advanced tonight to Clarksburg and joined [Benjamin S.] Roberts. They will fight to-day, or the rebels must run."

Governor Curtin's reply to Lincoln's telegram was received at 1:45 P.M.: "I have no doubt my dispatch to Pittsburg . . . sent since yours rec[eive]d will quiet the excitement in western Penn[sylvaniz]a. All the movements of the Government are perfectly satisfactory & your conclusion as to calling militia force in harmony with my views. I have not been seriously alarmed & in my despatches only reflected a part of the excitement & all from west."

Major-General Hooker:

Washington, D.C.,
May 4, 1863 (3:10 P.M.)

We have news here that the enemy has reoccupied heights above Fredericksburg. Is that so?

A. Lincoln

Telegram to General Joseph Hooker, May 4, 1863

Hon. Sec. of War. &
Genl. in-Chief.

Executive Mansion,
Washington, May 29. 1863.

I concur with Gov. Curtin and Gen. Schenck that an increased Cavalry force upon & South of the Baltimore and Ohio Railroad, is very desirable. Please see them, and if you can devise an eligible mode of getting such force, let it be done.

Yours truly
A. Lincoln

Communication to Secretary of War Edwin M. Stanton and General Henry W. Halleck, May 29, 1863

On May 18, General Schenck wrote Governor Curtin as follows:

"My conviction is briefly this: The only sure way to defend and guard the border is to keep all rebel forces out of West Virginia, or, rather, out of all the northern portion of Virginia, and this can only be done by a sufficient force of cavalry, to be kept south of the Baltimore and Ohio Railroad. The late rebel raid . . . should be a lesson. . . ." "Cavalry is, I repeat, needed; 10,000 well-mounted men would give more effective security than three times the number of infantry."

"I have represented time and again to the military authorities at Washington my want . . . but it occurs to me to endeavor to enlist your efforts also, as the Executive of your great State, so much concerned in the endeavor to have this command supplied with more of this arm of defense and aggression. Will you co-operate with me? . . ."

Washington, D.C.,
June 5. 1863

Major General Hooker

Yours of to-day was received an hour ago. So much of professional military skill is requisite to answer it, that I have turned the task over to Gen. Halleck. He promises to perform it with his utmost care. I have but one idea which I think worth suggesting to you, and that is in case you find Lee coming to the North of the Rappahannock, I would by no means cross to the South of it. If he should leave a rear force at Fredericksburg, tempting you to fall upon it, it would fight in intrenchments, and have you at disadvantage, and so, man for man, worst you at that point, while his main force would in some way be getting an advantage of you Northward. In one word, I would not take any risk of being entangled upon the river, like an ox jumped half over a fence, and liable to be torn by dogs, front and rear, without a fair chance to gore one way or kick the other. If Lee would come to my side of the river, I would keep on the same side & fight him, or act on the defence, according as might be my estimate of his strength relatively to my own. But these are mere suggestions which I desire to be controlled by the judgment of yourself and Gen. Halleck.

A. Lincoln

TELEGRAM TO GENERAL JOSEPH HOOKER, JUNE 5, 1863

HOOKER'S TELEGRAM OF JUNE 5, IS AS FOLLOWS:

"YESTERDAY MORNING APPEARANCES INDICATED THAT DURING THE NIGHT THE ENEMY HAD BROKEN UP A FEW OF HIS CAMPS AND ABANDONED THEM. THESE CHANGES WERE OBSERVED ON THE RIGHT OF HIS LINE IN THE VICINITY OF HAMILTON CROSSING. SO FAR AS I WAS ENABLED TO JUDGE FROM ALL MY MEANS OF INFORMATION IT WAS IMPOSSIBLE FOR ME TO DETERMINE SATISFACTORILY WHETHER THIS MOVEMENT HAD BEEN MERELY A CHANGE OF CAMPS—THE ENEMY HAD MOVED IN THE DIRECTION OF RICHMOND, OR UP THE RIVER, BUT TAKEN IN CONNECTION WITH THE FACT THAT SOME DESERTERS CAME IN FROM THE DIVISIONS OF [JOHN B.] HOOD AND [GEORGE] PICKETT I CONCLUDE THAT THOSE DIVISIONS HAD BEEN BROUGHT TO THE FRONT FROM THEIR LATE POSITIONS AT GORDONSVILLE AND TAYLORVILLE AND THAT THIS COULD BE FOR NO OTHER PURPOSE BUT TO ENABLE THE ENEMY TO MOVE UP THE RIVER WITH A VIEW TO THE EXECUTION OF A MOVEMENT SIMILAR TO THAT OF LEE'S LAST YEAR. HE MUST EITHER HAVE IT IN MIND TO CROSS THE UPPER POTOMAC OR TO THROW HIS ARMY BETWEEN MINE AND WASHINGTON. IN CASE I AM CORRECT IN MY CONJECTURE, TO ACCOMPLISH EITHER HE MUST HAVE BEEN GREATLY REINFORCED AND, IF MAKING THIS MOVEMENT, THE FAIR PRESUMPTION IS THAT HE HAS BEEN BY THE TROOPS FROM CHARLESTON . . . ."

Marye's Heights, and the stone wall at the base of the hill, was a heavily fortified position across the Rappahannock River (Fredericksburg National Battlefield). Two months before Gettysburg, Lincoln was concerned Hooker would repeat the blunder made at Fredericksburg the previous winter.

Although he probably should have removed Hooker, Lincoln hesitated to do so. When General John Reynolds, in command of the Second Corps, denounced Fighting Joe, Lincoln replied "that he was not disposed to throw away a gun because it missed fire once" and that "he would pick the flint and try it again." To Hooker's plea not to be removed, Lincoln assured him: "I am satisfied with your conduct. I tried McClellan twenty times; I see no reason why I can't try you at least twice." Lincoln probably worried that the abrupt removal of Hooker would undermine public confidence in the administration.

On June 2, Lincoln explained to a caller who feared that the Confederates might strike northward "that all indications were that there would be nothing of the sort, and that an advance by the rebels could not possibly take place so as to put them on this side of the Rappahannock unless Hooker was very much mistaken, and was to be again out-generaled." But soon thereafter, Lee, in fact, launched his second invasion of the North, driving along the Shenandoah Valley into Maryland, just as he had done several months earlier, only to be checked at the Battle of Antietam.

On June 5, in response to Hooker's proposal to attack the Confederate rear at Fredericksburg, Lincoln recommended that he focus on the main body of the Army of Northern Virginia: "in case you find Lee coming to the North of the Rappahannock, I would by no means cross to the South of it. If he should leave a rear force at Fredericksburg, tempting you to fall upon it, it would fight in intrenchments, and have you at disadvantage, and so, man for man, worst you at that point, while his main force would in some way be getting an advantage of you Northward." He urged Hooker to avoid "any risk of being entangled upon the river, like an ox jumped half over a fence, and liable to be torn by dogs, front and rear, without a fair chance to gore one way or kick the other." If Lee crossed the river, Hooker should "keep on the same side & fight him, or act on the defence, according as might be my estimate of his strength relatively to my own." Lincoln modestly ended his advice declaring that "these are mere suggestions which I desire to be controlled by the judgment of yourself and Gen[eral Henry W.] Halleck [general in chief of the Union armies] ."

On June 10, when Hooker proposed to march on Richmond, Lincoln vetoed that suggestion, for he thought "it would be a very poor exchange" to give up Washington for the Confederate capital. "If left to me," he counseled Hooker, "I would not go South of the Rappahannock, upon Lee's moving North of it. If you had Richmond invested to-day, you would not be able to take it in twenty days; meanwhile, your communications, and with them, your army would be ruined. I think Lee's Army, and not Richmond, is your true objective point. If he comes towards the Upper Potomac, follow on his flank, and on the inside track, shortening your lines, whilst he lengthens his. Fight him when oppertunity offers. If he stays where he is, fret him, and fret him."

"CYPHER"

Major General Hooker

June 10. 1863. (6:40 P.M.)

Your long despatch of to-day is just received. If left to me, I would not go South of the Rappahannock, upon Lee's moving North of it. If you had Richmond invested to-day, you would not be able to take it in twenty days; meanwhile, your communications, and with them, your army would be ruined. I think Lee's Army, and not Richmond, is your true objective point. If he comes towards the Upper Potomac, follow on his flank, and on the inside track, shortening your lines, whilst he lengthens his. Fight him when opportunity offers. If he stays where he is, fret him, and fret him.

A. Lincoln

TELEGRAM TO GENERAL JOSEPH HOOKER, JUNE 10, 1863

Washington, June 14, 1863 (5:50 P.M.)

Major-General Hooker: So far as we can make out here, the enemy have Milroy surrounded at Winchester, and Tyler at Martinsburg. If they could hold out a few days, could you help them? If the head of Lee's army is at Martinsburg and the tail of it on the Plank road between Fredericksburg and Chancellorsville, the animal must be very slim somewhere. Could you not break him?

A. Lincoln

TELEGRAM TO GENERAL JOSEPH HOOKER, JUNE 14, 1863

Major General Hooker.

Yours of 11.30 just received. You have nearly all the elements for forming an opinion whether Winchester is surrounded that I have. I really fear—almost believe, it is. No communication has been had with it during the day, either at Martinsburg, or Harper's Ferry. At 7 P.M., we also lost communication with Martinsburg. The enemy had also appeared there some hours before. At 9. P.M. Harper's Ferry said the enemy was reported at Berryville & Smithfield. If I could know that Longstreet and Ewell moved in that direction so long ago as you stated in your last, then I should feel sure that Winchester is strongly invested. It is quite certain that a considerable force of the enemy is thereabout; and I fear it is an overwhelming one, compared with Milroy's. I am unable to give any more certain opinion.

A. Lincoln

TELEGRAM TO GENERAL JOSEPH HOOKER, JUNE 14, 1863

Major General Hooker
Fairfax Station.

The facts are now known here that Winchester and Martinsburg were both besieged yesterday; the troops from Martinsburg have got into Harper's Ferry without loss; those from Winchester, are also in, having lost, in killed, wounded and missing, about one third of their number. Of course the enemy holds both places; and I think the report is authentic that he is crossing the Potomac at Williamsburg. We have not heard of his yet appearing at Harper's Ferry, or on the river anywhere below. I would like to hear from you.

A. Lincoln

TELEGRAM TO GENERAL JOSEPH HOOKER, JUNE 15, 1863

Washington, D.C.
June 16, 1863.

Major General Hooker:

Your despatches of last night and this morning are just received. I shall have General Halleck to answer them carefully. Meanwhile, I can only say that, as I understand, Heintzelman commands here in this District; that what troops, or very nearly what number, are at Harper's Ferry I do not know, though I do know that Tyler is in command there. Your idea to send your cavalry to this side of the river may be right—probably is; still, it pains me a little that it looks like defensive merely, and seems to abandon the fair chance now presented of breaking the enemy's long and necessarily slim line, stretched now from the Rappahannock to Pennsylvania.

A. Lincoln

TELEGRAM TO GENERAL JOSEPH HOOKER, JUNE 16, 1863

(PRIVATE.)

EXECUTIVE MANSION,
WASHINGTON, D.C., June 16, 1863.

My dear General: I send you this by the hand of Captain Dahlgren. Your despatch of 11:30 A. M. to-day is just received. When you say I have long been aware that you do not enjoy the confidence of the major-general commanding, you state the case much too strongly.

You do not lack his confidence in any degree to do you any harm. On seeing him, after telegraphing you this morning, I found him more nearly agreeing with you than I was myself. Surely you do not mean to understand that I am withholding my confidence from you when I happen to express an opinion (certainly never discourteously) differing from one of your own.

CONTINUED ON PAGE 19:

Continued from page 18:

I believe Halleck is dissatisfied with you to this extent only, that he knows that you write and telegraph ("report," as he calls it) to me. I think he is wrong to find fault with this; but I do not think he withholds any support from you on account of it. If you and he would use the same frankness to one another, and to me, that I use to both of you, there would be no difficulty. I need and must have the professional skill of both, and yet these suspicions tend to deprive me of both.

I believe you are aware that since you took command of the army I have not believed you had any chance to effect anything till now. As it looks to me, Lee's now returning toward Harper's Ferry gives you back the chance that I thought McClellan lost last fall. Quite possibly I was wrong both then and now; but, in the great responsibility resting upon me, I cannot be entirely silent. Now, all I ask is that you will be in such mood that we can get into our action the best cordial judgment of yourself and General Halleck, with my poor mite added, if indeed he and you shall think it entitled to any consideration at all.

Yours as ever,

A. Lincoln

TELEGRAM TO GENERAL JOSEPH HOOKER, JUNE 16, 1863

EXECUTIVE MANSION,

WASHINGTON, June 16. 1863. (10:00 P.M.)

Major General Hooker.

To remove all misunderstanding, I now place you in the strict military relation to Gen. Halleck, of a commander of one of the armies, to the General-in-Chief of all the armies. I have not intended differently; but as it seems to be differently understood, I shall direct him to give you orders, and you to obey them.

A. Lincoln

TELEGRAM TO GENERAL JOSEPH HOOKER, JUNE 16, 1863

Hooker eventually accepted that advice and shadowed the Confederates as they marched north. In time, Lincoln began to think that Fighting Joe was not eager for battle, despite his sobriquet. On June 16, the general wired Lincoln: "You have long been aware, Mr. President, that I have not enjoyed the confidence of the major-general commanding the army [Halleck], and I can assure you so long as this continues we may look in vain for success."

Lincoln responded firmly: "To remove all misunderstanding, I now place you in the strict military relation to Gen. Halleck, of a commander of one of the armies, to the General-in-Chief of all the armies. I have not intended differently; but as it seems to be differently understood, I shall direct him to give you orders, and you to obey them."

In a more conciliatory letter, Lincoln told Hooker: "When you say I have long been aware that you do not enjoy the confidence of the major-general commanding, you state the case much too strongly. You do not lack his confidence in any degree to do you any harm. On seeing him, after telegraphing you this morning, I found him more nearly agreeing with you than I was myself. Surely you do not mean to understand that I am withholding my confidence from you when I happen to express an opinion (certainly never discourteously) differing from one of your own. I believe Halleck is dissatisfied with you to this extent only, that he knows that you write and telegraph ('report,' as he calls it) to me. I think he is wrong to find fault with this; but I do not think he withholds any support from you on account of it. If you and he would use the same frankness to one another, and to me, that I use to both of you, there would be no difficulty. I need and must have the professional skill of both, and yet these suspicions tend to deprive me of both. I believe you are aware that since you took command of the army I have not believed you had any chance to effect anything till now. As it looks to me, Lee's now returning toward Harper's Ferry gives you back the chance that I thought McClellan lost last fall. Quite possibly I was wrong both then and now; but, in the great responsibility resting upon me, I cannot be entirely silent. Now, all I ask is that you will be in such mood that we can get into our action the best cordial judgment of yourself and General Halleck, with my poor mite added, if indeed he and you shall think it entitled to any consideration at all."

Despite his anxiety about Hooker's seeming timidity, Lincoln strove to remain optimistic. On June 26, he said: "We cannot help beating them, if we have the man. How much depends in military matters on one master mind! Hooker may commit the same fault as McClellan and lose his chance. We shall soon see, but it appears to me he can't help but win."

When, however, Halleck rejected Hooker's request that troops guarding Harpers Ferry be sent to his army, Fighting Joe on June 27 impulsively resigned his command. Upon reading Hooker's dispatch, which Secretary of War Edwin M. Stanton gave him, Lincoln turned ashen.

To Stanton's query: "What shall be done?" he responded: "Accept his resignation."

View from the Maryland bank as fog hangs in the Virginia Blue Ridge over the Potomac River at Harpers Ferry National Historical Park.

The Confederate States Army plundered farms and towns across Pennsylvania during the Gettysburg Campaign. On June 26, Jubal Early's division of approximately 5,500 Confederates, marched into Gettysburg. The Confederates demanded a ransom, which was never paid. After terrifying the residents of the borough, the Confederate forces left early the next morning for York, Pennsylvania, which did pay a large ransom of cash, food, clothing, and shoes.

When Secretary of the Treasury Salmon P. Chase, a strong supporter of Hooker, protested, Lincoln abruptly put him in his place: "The acceptance of an army resignation is not a matter for your department."

A replacement for Hooker had to be chosen swiftly, presumably a corps commander in the Army of the Potomac. Darius Couch declined, pleading poor health. Though John F. Reynolds had complained heatedly about Hooker, he refused to take over from him. Winfield Scott Hancock and John Sedgwick showed no interest in assuming command of the army. By default the administration settled on George Gordon Meade, who had a sterling record. When he heard that Meade was from Pennsylvania, Lincoln quipped that, like a gamecock, the general would probably "fight well on his own dunghill." Troops referred to him as "a damned old goggle-eyed snapping turtle." Though an industrious, fearless officer who commanded the respect of his fellow corps commanders, he had no charisma and was "conservative and cautious to the last degree, good qualities in a defensive general, but liable to degenerate into timidity when an aggressive or bold offensive becomes imperative."

Meanwhile, Lee had divided his forces as he penetrated into Maryland and Pennsylvania unopposed. Upon realizing that the Union army was pursuing him in earnest, he decided to concentrate them. On the morning of July 1, as they streamed toward the small town of Gettysburg from both the north and the west, they encountered advance units of the Army of the Potomac. The first clash took place northwest of town, where a dismounted cavalry division under Union General John Buford deployed along Herr Ridge, McPherson Ridge, and Seminary Ridge. Armed with breech-loading carbines, the Union troopers managed to slow down the advance of the larger Confederate forces under General Harry Heth for a few hours, long enough for infantry of John Reynold's corps to arrive and support them. As the fighting raged, Reynolds – arguably the ablest general in the Army of the Potomac – was killed near McPherson's Woods. As the day wore on, more and more Confederate troops arrived and drove the Yankees back through the campus of the Lutheran Theological Seminary and the streets of the town.

Meanwhile, as Confederate General Richard Ewell's corps approached Gettysburg from the north, it encountered Union troops of the freshly-arrived Eleventh Corps under Oliver Otis Howard. The outnumbered Federals were soon flanked and, like their comrades to the west, retreated south of town. There they occupied strategically crucial high ground: Culp's Hill, Cemetery Hill (where months later Lincoln would deliver the Gettysburg Address), and Cemetery Ridge.

Though the Union forces, representing about one quarter of the Army of the Potomac, were driven from the field by about one third of Lee's army, they had achieved an important advantage, for the terrain south of Gettysburg provided ideal defensive positions from which they would repel determined Confederate assaults over the next two days.

FROM ALONG THE EMMITSBURG ROAD DURING THE FIRST WEEK OF JULY, THE SUN SETS IN THE DIRECTION OF CASHTOWN, EIGHT MILES WEST AT THE BASE OF THE MOUNTAIN. FOR SEVERAL DAYS BEFORE THE BATTLE, THE WEATHER WAS HUMID, TYPICAL OF SUMMER. ON JUNE 30, THE EVE OF THE BATTLE, THERE WAS A BRILLIANT SUNSET IN THE WESTERN SKY OVER SOUTH MOUNTAIN.

OVER THE NEXT 24 HOURS, APPROXIMATELY 90,000-97,000 SOLDIERS OF THE ARMY OF THE POTOMAC AND APPROXIMATELY 70,000-75,000 SOLDIERS OF THE ARMY OF NORTHERN VIRGINIA WOULD DESCEND UPON THE SMALL COMMUNITY OF GETTYSBURG.

THE PRESIDENT'S HOUSE AT GETTYSBURG COLLEGE (PENNSYLVANIA COLLEGE IN 1863) IS ONE OF ONLY TWO
BUILDINGS ON THE CAMPUS THAT DATE TO 1863. FOLLOWING THE BATTLE, THE BUILDING WAS A HOSPITAL.

Union signal officers used the cupola in Pennsylvania Hall on June 30 and on July 1, 1863.
On July 1, a professor at the college led Union officers to the cupola to observe the battlefield.
Pennsylvania Hall is the oldest building at Gettysburg College (Pennsylvania College in 1863).
Following the battle, the building was a hospital for several weeks.
(National Historic Landmark)

THE LAST LIGHT OF A JULY DAY ON THE CUPOLA OF SCHMUCKER HALL AT THE LUTHERAN THEOLOGICAL SEMINARY IN GETTYSBURG (OLD DORM AT GETTYSBURG THEOLOGICAL SEMINARY IN 1863). OLD DORM WAS USED AS A UNION OBSERVATORY ON JUNE 30. AN AREA NEAR THE BUILDING WAS USED BY UNION ARTILLERY ON JULY 1, PRIOR TO THE LAST STAND OF THE UNION 1ST CORPS ON SEMINARY RIDGE. (NATIONAL HISTORIC LANDMARK)

A full moon in July rises to the tree tops along the bottom of Big Round Top. On the evening of July 1, following the Union withdrawal through the town of Gettysburg, a full moon rose above the battlefield. Soldiers continued to pour in from every direction and soon, between 160,000-172,000 men would occupy the area.

That night and next day most of the rest of the Army of the Potomac's 90,000 troops arrived and took positions on those commanding heights, forming a line that resembled a fishhook. The barb of the hook was Culp's Hill (southeast of town), forming the army's extreme right. The line curved up to Cemetery Hill (due south of town) and bent sharply to the south for approximately two miles along Cemetery Ridge (the long shaft of the fishhook). The eye of the fishhook was formed by two hills — Little Round Top and Round Top — anchoring the army's left. (pages 36 & 37)

In a line running parallel to this fishhook, Lee posted his 70,000 men, mostly along Seminary Ridge, about a mile from the Union line. On the second day, he sent James Longstreet's corps to hit the Union left. On its long march into position, it unexpectedly encountered a salient in the Union line created when General Daniel Sickles incautiously moved his corps off Cemetery Ridge half a mile forward. Taking advantage of this blunder, Longstreet's men attacked the exposed Federal units and fought fiercely at a peach orchard, a wheat field, and a boulder-strewn area known as Devil's Den. Confederate units nearly carried the extreme end of the Union line – Little Round Top – where Union troops (notably the 20th Maine Regiment, under Joshua Lawrence Chamberlain) heroically repelled desperate Confederate charges.

To meet Longstreet's threat to his left flank, Meade shifted units from the center and right of the fishhook line. Confederate attempts to overrun the weakened positions on Culp's Hill and Cemetery Hill failed, as did the plan to turn the Union left.

Having unsuccessfully struck both Union flanks, Lee decided on July 3 to attack the Union center. But as a prelude that morning Confederates again assaulted Culp's Hill, where they were thrice repelled. Early that afternoon Lee sent 12,000 men, among them the division of General George Pickett, against the Union center. As those troops crossed hundreds of yards of open field, Union artillery and musketry cut them to pieces. The few who managed to breach the Union line at "the Angle" near a copse of trees were quickly thrown back. Pickett's failed charge brought the Confederate campaign to an ignominious conclusion.

Lincoln rejoiced at the Union victory but not at Meade's order congratulating his troops. The general declared that their mission was now to "drive from our soil every vestige of the presence of the invader." Upon reading this proclamation, Lincoln dropped his hands to his knees and radiated disappointment. In a voice full of anguish, he exclaimed: "Drive the invader from our soil! My God! Is that all?" Lincoln called it "a dreadful reminiscences of McClellan. The same spirit that moved McC. to claim a great victory because P[ennsylvani]a and M[arylan]d were safe." Frustrated, he asked: "Will our Generals never get that idea out of their heads? The whole country is our soil."

On July 6 Lincoln wrote to General Halleck: "I left the telegraph office a good deal dissatisfied. You know I did not like the phrase, in Orders, No. 68, I believe, 'Drive the invaders from our soil.' Since that, I see a dispatch from

UNION ARTILLERY POSITION ON EAST CEMETERY HILL WITH CULP'S HILL, THE NORTHERN END OF THE UNION LINE, IN THE BACKGROUND. THE CANNON IN THE FOREGROUND IS 77 YARDS FROM THE GATEHOUSE, AND IS BETWEEN 250 AND 280 YARDS FROM WHERE ABRAHAM LINCOLN WOULD LATER DELIVER THE GETTYSBURG ADDRESS.

From the south end of the Union stronghold on Little Round Top, the July sun goes down over South Mountain in the direction of Cashtown, nine miles west of this rocky high ground. The round tops are the highest point on the battlefield and the west slope of Little Round Top had been cleared of forest, an important Union advantage.

FIERY JULY SKIES OVER A UNION ARTILLERY POSITION ON THE NORTHERN END OF CEMETERY RIDGE, THE CENTER OF THE UNION LINE, WHERE IT JOINS CEMETERY HILL NORTH OF THE COPSE OF TREES (FAR LEFT). THIS POSITION IS OVERLOOKING THE BROAD VALLEY DOWN TO SEMINARY RIDGE. SOUTH MOUNTAIN CAN BE SEEN IN THE DISTANCE ON THE RIGHT AND THE CATOCTIN MOUNTAINS IN THE CENTER.

31

THE JULY SUN SETS OVER SOUTH MOUNTAIN IN THE DIRECTION OF CASHTOWN, EIGHT MILES WEST OF THIS LOCATION ON CEMETERY RIDGE, THE CENTER OF THE UNION LINE. CONTROLLING THE HIGH RIDGES WAS CRUCIAL TO THE UNION VICTORY.

THIS PERSPECTIVE OF LITTLE ROUND TOP ON AN EARLY JULY MORNING REVEALS
THE OBSTACLE THE ADVANCING CONFEDERATES FACED CLIMBING THE STEEP GRANITE HILL.

Soldiers' Home, Washington,
July 6, 1863 (7:00 P.M.)

Major-General Halleck: I left the telegraph office a good deal dissatisfied. You know I did not like the phrase, in Orders, No. 68, I believe, "Drive the invaders from our soil." Since that, I see a dispatch from General French, saying the enemy is crossing his wounded over the river in flats, without saying why he does not stop it, or even intimating a thought that it ought to be stopped. Still later, another dispatch from General Pleasonton, by direction of General Meade, to General French, stating that the main army is halted because it is believed the rebels are concentrating "on the road toward Hagerstown, beyond Fairfield," and is not to move until it is ascertained that the rebels intend to evacuate Cumberland Valley.

These things all appear to me to be connected with a purpose to cover Baltimore and Washington, and to get the enemy across the river again without a further collision, and they do not appear connected with a purpose to prevent his crossing and to destroy him. I do fear the former purpose is acted upon and the latter is rejected.

If you are satisfied the latter purpose is entertained and is judiciously pursued, I am content. If you are not so satisfied, please look to it.

Yours, truly,
A. Lincoln

COMMUNICATION TO GENERAL HENRY W. HALLECK, JULY 6, 1863

MAJOR GENERAL GEORGE G. MEADE 'S GENERAL ORDERS NO. 68, JULY 4, 1863, AFTER THANKING HIS ARMY FOR DEFEATING "AN ENEMY, SUPERIOR IN NUMBERS, AND FLUSHED WITH THE PRIDE OF A SUCCESSFUL INVASION," CONTINUED AS FOLLOWS: "OUR TASK IS NOT YET ACCOMPLISHED, AND THE COMMANDING GENERAL LOOKS TO THE ARMY FOR GREATER EFFORTS TO DRIVE FROM OUR SOIL EVERY VESTIGE OF THE PRESENCE OF THE INVADER. . . ." GENERAL ALFRED PLEASONTON TELEGRAPHED GENERAL WILLIAM H. FRENCH AT 11 A.M. ON JULY 6, "MAJOR-GENERAL MEADE DESIRES ME TO SAY, IN CONSEQUENCE OF A LARGE BODY OF THE ENEMY BEING CONCENTRATED ON THE ROAD TOWARD HAGERSTOWN, BEYOND FAIRFIELD, HE HAS SUSPENDED HIS OPERATIONS FOR THE PRESENT. INDICATIONS GO TO SHOW THAT HE INTENDS EVACUATING THE CUMBERLAND VALLEY, BUT IT IS NOT YET POSITIVELY ASCERTAINED. UNTIL SO ASCERTAINED, THE GENERAL DOES NOT FEEL JUSTIFIED IN LEAVING HERE AND MOVING DOWN TOWARD YOU."

"[THE ENEMY IS VERY MUCH CRIPPLED. THE GENERAL IS UNDER NO APPREHENSION OF THEIR ATTACKING YOU, PROVIDED YOUR CAVALRY KEEP A GOOD LOOKOUT, AND ARE KEPT WELL OUT TO YOUR FRONT AND FLANKS.]" THE BRACKETS ARE IN THE SOURCE, AND A FOOTNOTE EXPLAINS: "THE CLAUSE IN BRACKETS DOES NOT APPEAR IN THE TELEGRAM AS RECEIVED 4 P.M. AT THE WAR DEPARTMENT." HAD LINCOLN SEEN THE OMITTED PARAGRAPH, HE WOULD PROBABLY HAVE BEEN EVEN MORE DISPLEASED AT MEADE'S OBVIOUS INTENT TO LET LEE WITHDRAW.

The center of the Union line on Cemetery Ridge was the target on July 3 for the formidable Confederate assault known as Pickett's Charge. The infantry assault of 12,000 Confederates was preceded by the largest cannonade of the Civil War. The massive artillery bombardment of 140-160 Confederate and 80-100 Union cannons (the exact numbers are unclear) could be heard as far away as Harrisburg, and there are several claims that include cities much farther away. The Confederates briefly broke the Union line at "the Angle", at the tree in front of this cannon on the north end of Cemetery Ridge.

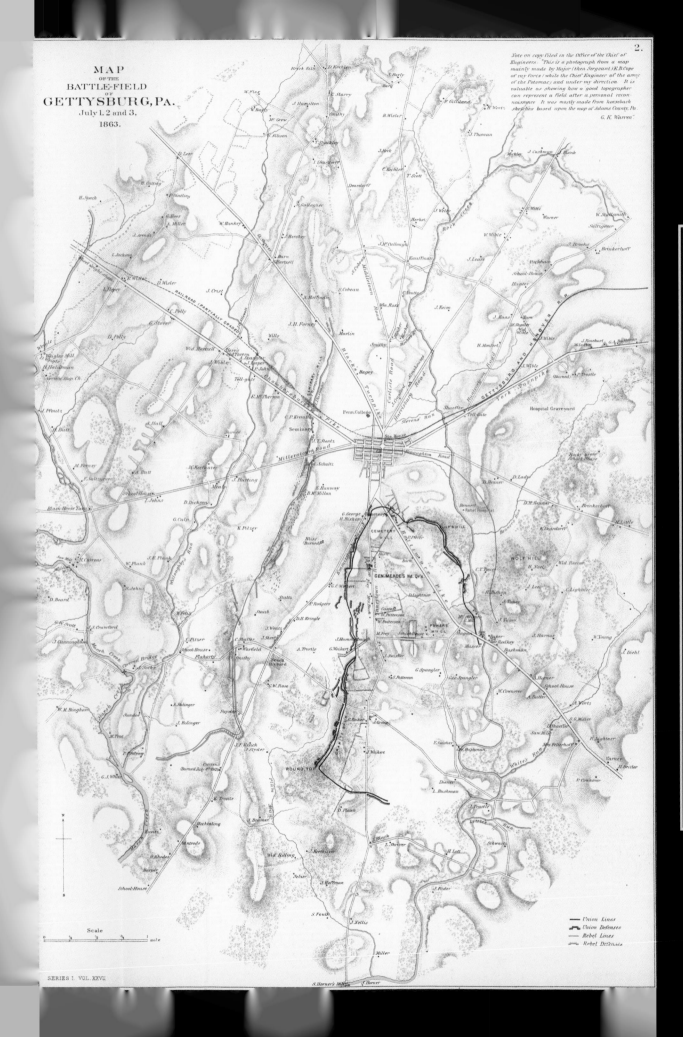

MAP
OF THE
BATTLE-FIELD
OF
GETTYSBURG, PA.
July 1, 2 and 3,
1863.

Note on copy filed in the Office of the Chief of Engineers: "This is a photograph from a map mainly made by Major (then Sergeant) R.B.Cope of my force (while the Chief Engineer of the army of the Potomac) and under my direction. It is valuable as showing how a good topographer can represent a field after a personal reconnaissance. It was mostly made from horseback sketches based upon the map of Adams County, Pa.

G. K. Warren

Legend:
— Union Lines
— Union Defenses
— Rebel Lines
— Rebel Defenses

Scale

MAPS OF GETTYSBURG BATTLEFIELD

Left:
author: United States War Department, 1895
full title: Map of the battle-field of Gettysburg, Pa. July 1, 2 and 3, 1863.
publisher: U.S. Government Printing Office, Washington

Right:
author: Brown, S. Howell; Confederate States of America. Army; Confederate States of America. Army of Northern Virginia, 1895
full title: Map of the battle-field of Gettysburg with positions of troops, July 2nd, 1863.
publisher: U.S. Government Printing Office, Washington

Source:
David Rumsey Historical Map Collection

ATLAS TO ACCOMPANY THE OFFICIAL RECORDS OF THE UNION AND CONFEDERATE ARMIES. 1861–1865.

1.

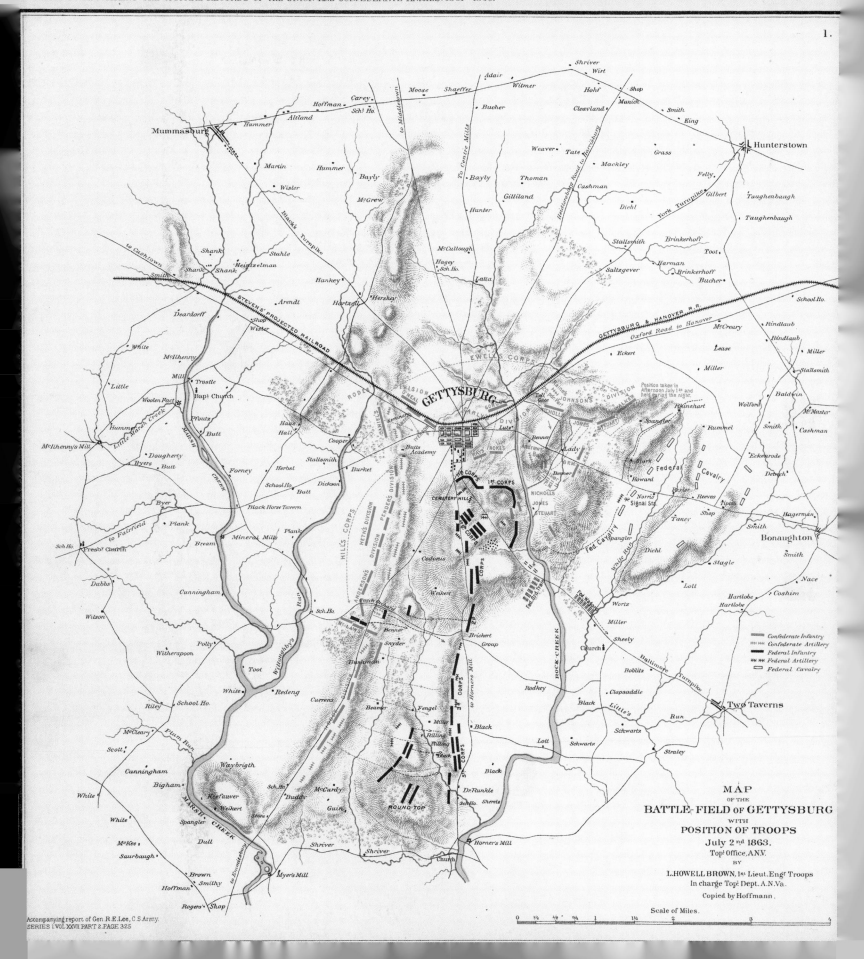

MAP
OF THE
BATTLE-FIELD of GETTYSBURG
WITH
POSITION OF TROOPS
July 2nd 1863.
Top! Office, A.N.V.
BY
L. HOWELL BROWN, 1st Lieut. Eng! Troops
In charge Top! Dept. A.N.Va.
Copied by Hoffmann.

Scale of Miles.

Confederate Infantry
Confederate Artillery
Federal Infantry
Federal Artillery
Federal Cavalry

A Union position on the south end of Cemetery Ridge during the first week of July.
Union cannons were firing nearly a mile across the fields to the Confederate line on Seminary Ridge on July 3.

General [William H.] French, saying the enemy is crossing his wounded over the river in flats, without saying why he does not stop it, or even intimating a thought that it ought to be stopped. Still later, another dispatch from General [Alfred] Pleasonton, by direction of General Meade, to General French, stating that the main army is halted because it is believed the rebels are concentrating 'on the road toward Hagerstown, beyond Fairfield,' and is not to move until it is ascertained that the rebels intend to evacuate Cumberland Valley. These things all appear to me to be connected with a purpose to cover Baltimore and Washington, and to get the enemy across the river again without a further collision, and they do not appear connected with a purpose to prevent his crossing and to destroy him. I do fear the former purpose is acted upon and the latter is rejected. If you are satisfied the latter purpose is entertained and is judiciously pursued, I am content. If you are not so satisfied, please look to it."

Lincoln thought that Meade could administer the coup de grâce to Lee's Army before it crossed the Potomac. Thus, he believed, Meade might end the war, in conjunction with U. S. Grant's capture of Vicksburg on July 4.

Halleck telegraphed Meade saying that if the Army of Northern Virginia was in the midst of crossing the Potomac, he should strike the units still north of the river: "the importance of attacking the part on this side is incalculable. Such an opportunity may not occur again."

Even if the entire Confederate Army was still on northern soil, Halleck told Meade: "You will have forces sufficient to render your victory certain. My only fear now is that the enemy may escape by crossing the river." Halleck added: "Do not be influenced by any dispatch from here against your own judgment. Regard them as suggestions only."

Meade replied: "I expect to find the enemy in a strong position, well covered with artillery. I do not desire to imitate his example at Gettysburg, and assault a position where the chances were so greatly against success. I wish in advance to moderate the expectations of those who, in ignorance of the difficulties to be encountered, may expect too much. All that I can do under the circumstances, I pledge this army to do."

Over the next few days Lincoln practically lived at the War Department, where a telegrapher observed him closely. Lincoln's "anxiety seemed as great as it had been during the battle itself," the telegrapher recalled; the President "walked up and down the floor, his face grave and anxious, wringing his hands and showing every sign of deep solicitude. As the telegrams came in, he traced the positions of the two armies on the map, and several times called me up to point out their location, seeming to feel the need of talking to some one. Finally, a telegram came from Meade saying that under such and such circumstances he would engage the enemy at such and such a time. 'Yes,' said the President bitterly, 'he will be ready to fight a magnificent battle when there is no enemy there to fight!'"

On July 7, the deeply discouraged President told his cabinet "that Meade still lingered at Gettysburg, when he should have been at Hagerstown or near the Potomac, to cut off the retreating army of Lee. While unwilling to complain and willing and anxious to give all praise to the general for the great battle and victory, he feared the old idea of driving the Rebels out of Pennsylvania and Maryland, instead of capturing them, was still prevalent among the officers. He hoped this was not so" and "said he had spoken to Halleck and urged that the right tone and sprit should be infused into officers and men," and that Meade "especially should be reminded of his . . . wishes." When Halleck responded with "a short and curt reply," Lincoln said: "I drop the subject." He thought he must yield to Halleck: "It being strictly a military question, it is proper I should defer to Halleck, whom I have called here to counsel, advise, and direct in these matters, where he is an expert."

In frustration, Lincoln penned a desperate order. His son Robert remembered that he "summoned Gen. [Herman] Haupt, in whom he had great Confidence as a bridge builder, and asked him how long in view of the materials which might be . . . available to General Lee, would it take him to devise the means and get his army across the river." Haupt calculated that it would take no more than twenty-four hours. The President "at once sent an order to Gen. Meade," a document probably carried north by Vice President Hannibal Hamlin, "directing him to attack Lee's army with all his force immediately, and that if he was successful in the attack he might destroy the order but if he was unsuccessful he might preserve it for his vindication."

On July 12, Meade caught up with Lee at Williamsport, Pennsylvania. When he wired that he intended to convene a council of war, Halleck replied: "Call no council of war. It is proverbial that councils of war never fight." Meade spurned this advice, and as Halleck had anticipated, most of the corps commanders advised against an attack. The Army of Northern Virginia crossed the Potomac unmolested on July 14.

When news of this development reached Lincoln, his "grief and anger were something sorrowful to behold," according to the messenger who delivered the bad news. On July 14, assistant presidential secretary John Hay recorded in his diary: "This morning the Presdt seemed depressed by Meade's dispatches of last night. They were so cautiously & almost timidly worded – talking about reconnoitering to find the enemy's weak place and other such." Lincoln "said he feared he would do nothing." Around midday, when Lee's escape was confirmed, the "deeply grieved" President said: "We only had to stretch forth our hands & they were ours. And nothing I could say or do could make the Army move." Robert Lincoln reported that his father "grieved silently but deeply about the escape of Lee. He said, 'If I had gone up there I could have whipped them myself.'" For the first and only time, Robert observed tears well up in his father's eyes.

Halleck wired Meade: "I need hardly say to you that the escape of Lee's army without another battle has created

THE EVERGREEN CEMETERY GATEHOUSE WAS NEAR THE CENTER OF THE BATTLE ON CEMETERY HILL. DURING AN INFANTRY ASSAULT ON JULY 2, THE CONFEDERATES CAME WITHIN LESS THAN A HUNDRED YARDS OF THE GATEHOUSE WHEN THEY BROKE THE UNION LINE ON EAST CEMETERY HILL FOR A SHORT PERIOD OF TIME. THE GATEHOUSE IS LOCATED ON THE BALTIMORE PIKE, ONE OF TEN ROADS LEADING INTO GETTYSBURG. ON JULY 2 AND 3, THE UNION ARMY CONTROLLED ONLY TWO OF THE TEN ROADS—ONE OF THEM WAS THE BALTIMORE PIKE, THE UNION'S MAIN SUPPLY LINE.

expect, and I do not expect you can now effect much. Your golden opportunity is gone, and I am distressed immeasureably because of it."

Lincoln filed away this remarkable letter with the endorsement: "To Gen. Meade, never sent, or signed." But he did tell the general, "The fruit seemed so ripe, so ready for plucking, that it was very hard to lose it."

The following day Lincoln wrote: "I would give much to be relieved of the impression that Meade, Couch, Smith and all, since the battle of Gettysburg, have striven only to get Lee over the river without another fight." A week later, Lincoln was in a better frame of mind. "I was deeply mortified by the escape of Lee," he told one of Meade's corps commanders. "A few days having passed," he added, "I am now profoundly grateful for what was done, without criticism for what was not done."

Nevertheless, Lincoln continued to deplore Meade's caution. On July 18, he told Hay: "Our Army had the war in the hollow of their hand & they would not close it . . . . We had gone through all the labor of tilling & planting an enormous crop & when it was ripe we did not harvest it." He feared that Meade wanted the Confederates to slip back into Virginia unharmed.

Later, the President asked Meade: "Do you know, General, what your attitude towards Lee after the battle of Gettysburg reminded me of?"

"No, Mr. President – what is it?"

"I'll be hanged if I could think of anything but an old woman trying to shoo her geese across the creek."

"There is bad faith somewhere," Lincoln speculated to Gideon Welles. "Meade has been pressed and urged, but only one of his generals was for an immediate attack. . . . What does it mean, Mr. Welles? Great God! what does it mean." On July 26, he told Welles: "I have no faith that Meade will attack Lee; nothing looks like it to me. I believe he can never have another as good opportunity as that which he trifled away. Everything since has dragged with him." In September, when asked what Meade was doing, Lincoln replied: "It is the same old story of this Army of the Potomac. Imbecility, inefficiency – don't want to do – is defending the Capital." He moaned, "Oh, it is terrible, terrible this weakness, this indifference of our Potomac generals, with such armies of good and brave men."

Others shared Lincoln's belief that Meade could have ended the war with a vigorous pursuit. "Had Meade finished Lee before he had crossed the Potomac, as he might have done & he should have done, . . . we should now be at the end of the war," wrote Charles A. Dana on July 29. Journalist Whitelaw Reid called Lee's escape "the greatest blunder of the war," and Supreme Court Justice David Davis deemed it "one of the great disasters & humiliations of the war."

In fact, if Meade had begun pursuing the Army of Northern Virginia by July 8, Lee may well have been forced to surrender. If U. S. Grant or Philip Sheridan had been in Meade's place, Lee would probably not have escaped.

Despite his keen disappointment, Lincoln on July 19 felt cheerful enough to pen a bit of doggerel titled "Gen. Lee[']s invasion of the North written by himself":

"In eighteen sixty three, with pomp, and mighty swell,
Me and Jeff's Confederacy, went forth to sack Phil-del,
The Yankees they got arter us, and giv us particular hell,
And we skedaddled back again, and didn't sack Phil-del."

In assessing credit for the victory at Gettysburg, Lincoln expressed reluctance to single out anyone in particular. "There was glory enough at Gettysburg to go all round, from Meade to the humblest man in the ranks," he told Daniel Sickles.

HEAVILY WOODED BIG ROUND TOP (IN THE DISTANCE) AS VIEWED FROM THE SOUTH SIDE OF LITTLE ROUND TOP. THE LARGE HILLS ARE ACTUALLY ONE GEOLOGIC GRANITE STRUCTURE WITH A SADDLE IN BETWEEN.

BOULDERS AT SPANGLER'S SPRING AT THE SOUTH BASE OF CULP'S HILL. THE AREA AROUND CULP'S HILL SAW LONG,
INTENSE BATTLES WHICH INCLUDED SOME OF THE FIERCEST NIGHT FIGHTING IN THE CIVIL WAR.
JULY 2 SAW INTENSE BATTLES ON BOTH ENDS OF THE UNION LINE—FROM CULP'S HILL TO LITTLE ROUND TOP.

The heights of Little Round Top secured the south end of the Union line. On July 2, fighting raged on Little Round Top and much of the surrounding area on the south end of the Union line. On July 2, fighting also roared on the north end of the line throughout the Culp's Hill area, including East Cemetery Hill.

CASUALTIES WERE VERY HEAVY IN THE AREA KNOWN AS THE WHEATFIELD.
THE NORTH EDGE OF THE FIELD BORDERS ALONG THE MILLERSTOWN ROAD, THE ONLY ROAD
CONNECTING THE TANEYTOWN AND EMMITSBURG ROADS ON THE BATTLEFIELD, SOUTH OF THE TOWN.

At the Wheatfield in July, goldenrod now grows where wheat grew in 1863.

Union cannons on East Cemetery Hill were aimed at the valley below on the second and third day of the battle. Culp's Hill is in the distance, where heavy fighting raged on July 2, late into the night, and the morning of July 3.

THIS IS SIMILAR TO THE VIEW SOME CONFEDERATES HAD DURING AN ATTACK ON THE LATE AFTERNOON OF JULY 2,
COMING UP THE SLOPE OF EAST CEMETERY HILL AGAINST HEAVY CANNON FIRE. THE EVERGREEN CEMETERY
GATEHOUSE HAS DEVELOPED AN ICONIC PRESENCE ON TOP OF CEMETERY HILL SINCE THE BATTLE.

This area on the south end of Cemetery Ridge saw heavy fighting on July 2. The following day, July 3, Lee's massive assault known as Pickett's Charge was taking aim at Cemetery Ridge.

This image and the preceding page were made late afternoon on July 3, 2013,
the 150th anniversary of Pickett's Charge, on the south end of Cemetery Ridge.

Executive Mansion,
Washington, July 21. 1863.

My dear General Howard

Your letter of the 18th. is received. I was deeply mortified by the escape of Lee across the Potomac, because the substantial destruction of his army would have ended the war, and because I believed, such destruction was perfectly easy—believed that Gen. Meade and his noble army had expended all the skill, and toil, and blood, up to the ripe harvest, and then let the crop go to waste. Perhaps my mortification was heightened because I had always believed—making my belief a hobby possibly—that the main rebel army going North of the Potomac, could never return, if well attended to; and because I was so greatly flattered in this belief, by the operations at Gettysburg. A few days having passed, I am now profoundly grateful for what was done, without criticism for what was not done. Gen. Meade has my confidence as a brave and skillful officer, and a true man.

Yours very truly

A. Lincoln

LETTER TO OLIVER O. HOWARD, JULY 21, 1863

GENERAL HOWARD'S LETTER OF JULY 18, MARKED "UNOFFICIAL" BY HOWARD, READS:

"HAVING NOTICED IN THE NEWSPAPERS CERTAIN STATEMENTS BEARING UPON THE BATTLES OF GETTYSBURG AND SUBSEQUENT OPERATIONS WHICH I DEEM CALCULATED TO CONVEY A WRONG IMPRESSION TO YOUR MIND, I WISH TO SUBMIT A FEW STATEMENTS. THE SUCCESSFUL ISSUE OF THE BATTLE OF GETTYSBURG WAS DUE MAINLY TO THE ENERGETIC OPERATIONS OF OUR PRESENT COMMANDING GENERAL PRIOR TO THE ENGAGEMENT AND TO THE MANNER IN WHICH HE HANDLED HIS TROOPS ON THE FIELD. THE RESERVES HAVE NEVER BEFORE DURING THE WAR BEEN THROWN IN AT JUST THE RIGHT MOMENT. . . . MOREOVER I HAVE NEVER SEEN A MORE HEARTY CO-OPERATION ON THE PART OF GENERAL OFFICERS AS SINCE GENERAL MEADE TOOK THE COMMAND."

"AS TO NOT ATTACKING THE ENEMY PRIOR TO LEAVING HIS STRONGHOLD BEYOND THE ANTIETAM IT IS BY NO MEANS CERTAIN THAT THE REPULSE OF GETTYSBURG MIGHT NOT HAVE BEEN TURNED UPON US; AT ANY RATE THE COMMANDING GENERAL WAS IN FAVOR OF AN IMMEDIATE ATTACK BUT WITH THE EVIDENT DIFFICULTIES IN OUR WAY THE UNCERTAINTY OF A SUCCESS AND THE STRONG CONVICTION OF OUR BEST MILITARY MINDS AGAINST THE RISK, I MUST SAY, THAT I THINK THE GENERAL ACTED WISELY."

"AS TO MY REQUEST TO MAKE A RECONNAISSANCE ON THE MORNING OF THE 14TH WHICH THE PAPERS STATE WAS REFUSED; THE FACTS ARE, THAT THE GENERAL HAD REQUIRED ME TO RECONNOITRE THE EVENING BEFORE AND GIVE MY OPINION AS TO THE PRACTICABILITY OF MAKING A LODGEMENT ON THE ENEMY'S LEFT, AND HIS ANSWER TO MY SUBSEQUENT REQUEST WAS, THAT THE MOVEMENTS HE HAD ALREADY ORDERED WOULD SUBSERVE THE SAME PURPOSE."

"WE HAVE, IF I MAY BE ALLOWED TO SAY IT, A COMMANDING GENERAL IN WHOM ALL THE OFFICERS, WITH WHOM I HAVE COME IN CONTACT, EXPRESS COMPLETE CONFIDENCE. I HAVE SAID THIS MUCH BECAUSE OF THE CENSURE AND OF THE MISREPRESENTATIONS WHICH HAVE GROWN OUT OF THE ESCAPE OF LEE'S ARMY."

HOWARD DOUBTLESS REFERRED TO A WASHINGTON DISPATCH OF JULY 17, ENTITLED "THE ESCAPE OF LEE'S ARMY," APPEARING IN THE NEW YORK TRIBUNE OF JULY 18.

An early July morning at a Union artillery position on the northern end of Cemetery Ridge, the center of the Union line, where it joins Cemetery Hill. "The Angle", the point where the Confederates breached the Union line during Pickett's Charge, is at the tree on the left. South Mountain can be seen in the distance.

EXECUTIVE MANSION,

WASHINGTON, *July 29, 1863.*

Major General Halleck:

Seeing Gen. Meade's despatch of yesterday to yourself, causes, me to fear that he supposes the government here is demanding of him to bring on a general engagement with Lee as soon as possible. I am claiming no such thing of him. In fact, my judgment is against it; which judgment, of course, I will yield if yours and his are the contrary. If he could not safely engage Lee at Williamsport, it seems absurd to suppose he can safely engage him now, when he has scarcely more than two thirds of the force he had at Williamsport, while it must be, that Lee has been re-inforced. True, I desired Gen. Meade to pursue Lee across the Potomac, hoping, as has proved true, that he would thereby clear the Baltimore and Ohio Railroad, and get some advantages by harrassing him on his retreat. These being past, I am unwilling he should now get into a general engagement on the impression that we here are pressing him; and I shall be glad for you to so inform him, unless your own judgment is against it.

Yours truly

A. Lincoln

COMMUNICATION TO GENERAL HENRY W. HALLECK, JULY 29, 1863

GENERAL MEADE TELEGRAPHED HALLECK AT 3 P.M. ON JULY 28:

"I AM MAKING EVERY EFFORT TO PREPARE THIS ARMY FOR AN ADVANCE. . . . I AM IN HOPES TO COMMENCE THE MOVEMENT TO-MORROW, WHEN I SHALL FIRST THROW OVER A CAVALRY FORCE TO FEEL FOR THE ENEMY, AND CROSS THE INFANTRY AS FAST AS POSSIBLE. . . ."

"NO RELIABLE INTELLIGENCE OF THE POSITION OF THE ENEMY HAS BEEN OBTAINED. HE PICKETS THE RAPPAHANNOCK FROM FREDERICKSBURG TO RAPPAHANNOCK STATION. THESE PICKETS, HOWEVER, SEEM TO BE MERE `LOOKOUTS,' TO WARN HIM OF MY APPROACH."

"CONTRADICTORY REPORTS . . . PLACE THE MAIN BODY, SOME AT GORDONSVILLE, OTHERS SAY AT STAUNTON AND CHARLOTTESVILLE, AND SOME ASSERT THE RETREAT HAS BEEN EXTENDED TO RICHMOND. MY OWN EXPECTATION IS THAT HE WILL BE FOUND BEHIND THE LINE OF THE RAPIDAN. . . ."

"P.S. 4 P.M.—A SCOUT JUST RETURNED . . . REPORTS THE ENEMY HAVE REPAIRED THE RAILROAD BRIDGE ACROSS THE RAPIDAN, AND ARE USING THE ROAD TO CULPEPER COURT-HOUSE; THAT LEE HAS BEEN RE-ENFORCED BY D. H. HILL, REPORTED WITH 10,000 MEN, AND THAT HE INTENDS TO MAKE A STAND AT CULPEPER OR IN ITS VICINITY."

AT 10 A.M., HALLECK COMMUNICATED LINCOLN'S NOTE TO MEADE.

THE TOTAL CASUALTIES FOR THE GETTYSBURG CAMPAIGN FROM MID-JUNE THROUGH MID-JULY WAS 51,000, WHICH INCLUDES THE 46,363+ INCURRED DURING THE THREE-DAY BATTLE OF GETTYSBURG. THE ACTUAL NUMBER OF CASUALTIES WILL NEVER BE KNOWN DUE TO INCOMPLETE RECORDS, BUT THERE ARE TWO DIFFERENT SOURCES HISTORIANS RELY UPON— THE OFFICIAL RECORDS AND THE FIGURES COMPILED BY RESEARCHER JOHN BUSEY, WHO DID MOST OF HIS WORK WITH INDIVIDUAL SERVICE FILES AT THE NATIONAL ARCHIVES. MOST HISTORIANS CONSIDER BUSEY'S CASUALTY FIGURES MORE ACCURATE. HE PUBLISHED HIS FINDINGS IN THE BOOK <u>REGIMENTAL STRENGTHS AND LOSSES AT GETTYSBURG</u>. JOHN BUSEY'S CASUALTY NUMBERS ARE:

ARMY OF THE POTOMAC - 23,806 CASUALTIES; 3,149 KILLED, 15,500 WOUNDED, 5,157 MISSING OR CAPTURED
ARMY OF NORTHERN VIRGINIA - 22,557 CASUALTIES; 4,559 KILLED, 12,355 WOUNDED, 5,643+ MISSING OR CAPTURED

FIGURES GIVEN IN REPORTS FILED IN THE OFFICIAL RECORDS OF THE UNION AND CONFEDERATE ARMIES ARE SLIGHTLY DIFFERENT, PRIMARILY WITH CONFEDERATE LOSSES SINCE THE ACCOUNTING SYSTEM THEY USED WAS INCOMPLETE. THE NUMBERS FROM THE OFFICIAL RECORDS ARE: ARMY OF THE POTOMAC - 23,049 CASUALTIES
ARMY OF NORTHERN VIRGINIA - 20,451 CASUALTIES

ABOVE: UNION CANNONS ON EAST CEMETERY HILL WITH CULP'S HILL IN THE DISTANCE.
AFTER THREE DAYS OF CARNAGE AND MANY THOUSANDS DEAD OR NEAR DEATH, THE GREAT BATTLE WAS OVER.

Lightning strikes on both pages were from separate July thunderstorms. These photographs were made at the crest of Little Round Top. With the failure of Lee's full-scale assault of July 3, the Confederates began to retreat. On July 4, storms with heavy rain inundated the region. Roads turned to mud, making for a difficult retreat for the Confederates.

THE CONFEDERATES MADE A SLOW RETREAT WITH MANY CASUALTIES. PRESIDENT LINCOLN URGED GENERAL MEADE TO SEIZE THE OPPORTUNITY TO DESTROY LEE'S ARMY WHILE THE CONFEDERATES WERE WEAKENED, PROBABLY LOW ON SUPPLIES, CUT OFF FROM REINFORCEMENTS, AND NORTH OF THE CROSSING ON THE POTOMAC RIVER—AT THE SAME TIME THE UNION ARMY HAD NEW REINFORCEMENTS, COULD MAINTAIN A STEADY SUPPLY LINE, AND HAD THE POTENTIAL TO TURN THE RIVER CROSSING INTO AN ADVANTAGE.

and so dedicated, can
on a great battle field
come to dedicate a port-
ing place for those who
might live. This we may, i
larger sense, we can not
consecrate— we can not
The brave men, living a
hers, have hallowed it,
to add or detract. The

long endure. We are met

of that war. We have

come of it, as a final rest-

ed here, that the nation

ale propriety do. But, in a

dedicate — we can not

hallow, this ground —

ned dead, who struggled

far above our poor power

world will little note, nor long

Fellow-citizens: I am very glad indeed to see you to-night, and yet I will not say I thank you for this call, but I do most sincerely thank Almighty God for the occasion on which you have called. [CHEERS.] How long ago is it?—eighty odd years—since on the Fourth of July for the first time in the history of the world a nation by its representatives, assembled and declared as a self-evident truth that "all men are created equal." [CHEERS.] That was the birthday of the United States of America. Since then the Fourth of July has had several peculiar recognitions. The two most distinguished men in the framing and support of the Declaration were Thomas Jefferson and John Adams—the one having penned it and the other sustained it the most forcibly in debate— the only two of the fifty-five who sustained it being elected President of the United States. Precisely fifty years after they put their hands to the paper it pleased Almighty God to take both from the stage of action. This was indeed an extraordinary and remarkable event in our history. Another President, five years after, was called from this stage of existence on the same day and month of the year; and now, on this last Fourth of July just passed, when we have a gigantic Rebellion, at the bottom of which is an effort to overthrow the principle that all men were created equal, we have the surrender of a most powerful position and army on that very day, [CHEERS] and not only so, but in a succession of battles in Pennsylvania, near to us, through three days, so rapidly fought that they might be called one great battle on the 1st, 2d and 3d of the month of July; and on the 4th the cohorts of those who opposed the declaration that all men are created equal, "turned tail" and run. [LONG AND CONTINUED CHEERS.] Gentlemen, this is a glorious theme, and the occasion for a speech, but I am not prepared to make one worthy of the occasion. I would like to speak in terms of praise due to the many brave officers and soldiers who have fought in the cause of the Union and liberties of the country from the beginning of the war. There are trying occasions, not only in success, but for the want of success. I dislike to mention the name of one single officer lest I might do wrong to those I might forget. Recent events bring up glorious names, and particularly prominent ones, but these I will not mention. Having said this much, I will now take the music.

EXTEMPORANEOUS SPEECH AT THE EXECUTIVE MANSION (RESPONSE TO A SERENADE), WASHINGTON, D.C., JULY 7, 1863—FOUR DAYS AFTER THE BATTLE OF GETTYSBURG.

PRESIDENT LINCOLN GAVE AN EXTEMPORANEOUS SPEECH OUTSIDE THE EXECUTIVE MANSION (THE WHITE HOUSE) ON JULY 7, 1863, AFTER LEARNING ABOUT THE VICTORIES AT BOTH GETTYSBURG AND VICKSBURG. THE SPEECH FORETELLS SEVERAL THOUGHTS LINCOLN WOULD LATER CAREFULLY ARTICULATE IN THE GETTYSBURG ADDRESS. HE BEGINS WITH HIS GREAT ASPIRATION FOR THE NATION.

EXECUTIVE MANSION,

WASHINGTON, *Nov. 9, 1863*

Dear Judge

Col. Lamon had made his calculation, as he tells me, to go to Illinois and bring Mrs. L. home this month, when he was called on to act as Marshal on the occasion of dedicating the Cemetery at Gettysburg Pa on the 19th. He came to me, and I told him I thought that in view of his relation to the government and to me, he could not well decline. Now, why would it not be pleasant for you to come on with Mrs. L. at that time? It will be an interesting ceremony, and I shall be very glad to see you. I know not whether you would care to remain to the meeting of congress, but that event, as you know, will be very near at hand.

Your friend as ever,

A. Lincoln

LETTER TO STEPHEN T. LOGAN, SPRINGFIELD, ILLINOIS, NOVEMBER 9, 1863

STEPHEN T. LOGAN WAS WARD H. LAMON'S FATHER-IN-LAW. LINCOLN APPOINTED LAMON UNITED STATES MARSHAL OF THE DISTRICT OF COLUMBIA IN 1861. LAMON SERVED AS LINCOLN'S PRIMARY BODYGUARD. AT THE DEDICATION OF THE SOLDIERS' NATIONAL CEMETERY IN GETTYSBURG, LAMON WAS "CALLED ON TO ACT AS MARSHAL ON THE OCCASION".

PAGE 69: THIS PORTRAIT OF ABRAHAM LINCOLN WAS MADE BY ALEXANDER GARDNER IN WASHINGTON, D.C., ON SUNDAY, NOVEMBER 8, 1863. LINCOLN WROTE THE LETTER ABOVE TO HIS OLD FRIEND IN SPRINGFIELD, ILLINOIS, THE DAY AFTER THIS PORTRAIT AND SEVERAL OTHERS WERE MADE AT GARDNER'S STUDIO.
(LLOYD OSTENDORF COLLECTION)

PRECEDING PAGE: THIS PORTRAIT OF PRESIDENT LINCOLN WAS MADE BY ALEXANDER GARDNER IN WASHINGTON, D.C., ON NOVEMBER 8, 1863. GARDNER MADE OVER THIRTY KNOWN PORTRAITS OF LINCOLN—MORE THAN ANY OTHER PHOTOGRAPHER.
(LLOYD OSTENDORF COLLECTION)

LINCOLN TRAVELS TO GETTYSBURG

There will be a train to take and return us.

COMMUNICATION TO SECRETARY OF THE TREASURY SALMON P. CHASE, NOVEMBER 17, 1863.
(ON NOVEMBER 18, CHASE DID NOT GO TO GETTYSBURG)

Lincoln told his good friend James Speed, who would become Attorney General of the U.S. in 1864, that "he was anxious to go" to Gettysburg, but as the ceremony date drew near, the President worried that he might not be able to do so, for he was reluctant to leave the bedside of his son Tad, ill with scarletina or perhaps smallpox. In addition, Ben: Perley Poore reported on November 14 that even though "it has been announced that the President will positively attend the inauguration of the Gettysburg soldiers' cemetery, it can hardly be possible for him to leave at this time, when his public duties are so pressing." (Among other things, Lincoln was paying close attention to military developments in Tennessee and was busy composing his annual message to Congress, to be delivered in early December.) But four days later, Poore wrote that "Such had been the pressure exerted on the President that he will probably go to Gettysburg tomorrow." The President did in fact depart for Pennsylvania on November 18 even though Tad's health remained questionable.

Accompanying Lincoln to Gettysburg were cabinet members (Secretary of State William Henry Seward, Interior Secretary John Palmer Usher, and Postmaster General Montgomery Blair), personal secretaries (John G. Nicolay and John Hay), a body servant (William Johnson), diplomatic representatives, Edward Everett's daughter and son-in-law (Mr. and Mrs. Henry Wise), and the Pennsylvania politician Wayne MacVeagh. Also aboard the four-coach train were bodyguards, journalists, and musicians. Secretary of War Edwin M. Stanton had originally arranged for the President to leave on the morning of the 19th, but Lincoln, fearing that was cutting it too close, insisted on departing the day before.

On November 18, 1863, a journalist traveling from Washington to Gettysburg wrote: "The approach to the town lies through a beautiful valley, studded with substantial homesteads, each adorned with the characteristic fine old German barn. Upon entering the town the hospital encampment on the right first indicates the approach to the theatre of the battle."

On Wednesday, November 18, President Lincoln departed the Executive Mansion (the White House) with a diverse entourage on a special four-coach train bound for Gettysburg, Pennsylvania.

I do not like this arrangement. I do not wish to so go that by the slightest accident we fail entirely, and, at the best, the whole to be a mere breathless running of the gauntlet. But, any way.

A. Lincoln

COMMUNICATION TO SECRETARY OF WAR EDWIN M. STANTON, NOVEMBER 17, 1863

NICOLAY AND HAY GIVE THIS AS AN ENDORSEMENT ON THE FOLLOWING LETTER FROM STANTON DATED NOVEMBER 17:

"MR. PRESIDENT: IT IS PROPOSED BY THE BALTIMORE AND OHIO ROAD—

FIRST, TO LEAVE WASHINGTON THURSDAY MORNING AT 6 A.M.; AND

SECOND, TO LEAVE BALTIMORE AT 8 A.M., ARRIVING AT GETTYSBURG AT 12 NOON, THUS GIVING TWO HOURS TO VIEW THE GROUND BEFORE THE DEDICATION CEREMONIES COMMENCE.

THIRD, TO LEAVE GETTYSBURG AT 6 P.M., AND ARRIVE IN WASHINGTON, MIDNIGHT; THUS DOING ALL IN ONE DAY.

MR. SMITH SAYS THE NORTHERN CENTRAL ROAD AGREES TO THIS ARRANGEMENT.

PLEASE CONSIDER IT, AND IF ANY CHANGE IS DESIRED, LET ME KNOW, SO THAT IT CAN BE MADE."

STANTON REPLIED LATER IN THE DAY: "THE ARRANGEMENT I PROPOSED HAS BEEN MADE. THE TRAIN WILL LEAVE THE DEPOT AT 12 O'CLOCK. I WILL ASSIGN THE ADJUTANT GENERAL OR COL. FRY TO ACCOMPANY YOU AS PERSONAL ESCORT AND TO CONTROL THE TRAIN. A CARRIAGE WILL CALL FOR YOU AT 12. PLEASE FURNISH ME THE NAMES OF THOSE WHOM YOU MAY INVITE THAT THEY MAY BE FURNISHED WITH TICKETS AND UNAUTHORIZED INTRUSION PREVENTED."

PRECEDING PAGE: THIS ICONIC PORTRAIT OF A CONFIDENT AND RESOLUTE ABRAHAM LINCOLN WAS MADE BY ALEXANDER GARDNER IN WASHINGTON, D.C., ON SUNDAY, NOVEMBER 8, 1863, ELEVEN DAYS BEFORE LINCOLN DELIVERED THE GETTYSBURG ADDRESS. DURING THIS PORTRAIT SESSION, GARDNER MADE SEVERAL PHOTOGRAPHS OF LINCOLN. THIS IS THE FULL-FRAME COMPOSITION OF THIS PORTRAIT. THE IMAGE IS USUALLY SEEN TIGHTLY CROPPED AS SHOWN ON PAGE 8.
(LLOYD OSTENDORF COLLECTION)

GETTYSBURG WELCOMES ABRAHAM LINCOLN

It will be an interesting ceremony, and I shall be very glad to see you.

LETTER TO STEPHEN T. LOGAN, SPRINGFIELD, ILLINOIS, NOVEMBER 9, 1863

Arriving in Gettysburg in the late afternoon of November 18, Lincoln, flanked by a cheering crowd, proceeded to the home of David Wills, where he was to spend the night. Edward Everett observed that at supper, the President was as gentlemanly in appearance, manners, and conversation as any of the diplomats, governors, and other eminenti at the table. Thus did Lincoln belie his reputation for backwoods social awkwardness. After the meal, serenaders regaled him at the Wills house. One of them recalled that the "appearance of the President was the signal for an outburst of enthusiasm that I had never heard equaled. When the people cheered and otherwise expressed their delight, he stood before us bowing his acknowledgments." He then asked to be excused from addressing them: "I appear before you, fellow-citizens, merely to thank you for this compliment. The inference is a very fair one that you would hear me for a little while at least, were I to commence to make a speech. I do not appear before you for the purpose of doing so, and for several substantial reasons. The most substantial of these is that I have no speech to make. [Laughter.] In my position it is somewhat important that I should not say any foolish things." An irreverent voice rang out: "If you can help it." Lincoln replied good-naturedly: "It very often happens that the only way to help it is to say nothing at all. [Laughter.] Believing that is my present condition this evening, I must beg of you to excuse me from addressing you further." The crowd greeted these remarks with "a tremendous outburst of applause" then moved next door to the home of Robert G. Harper, where Seward was staying. The secretary of state obliged them with more extensive remarks, strongly endorsing abolition and emphasizing that the war was fought to vindicate the principle of majority rule. This speech probably represents the formal remarks that Seward would have delivered at the ceremony in case Lincoln had remained in Washington.

Later that evening Lincoln greeted guests at a reception, then retired to work on his speech. Around 11 o'clock he stepped next door for an hour or so to confer with Seward about it. It is not known what, if any, suggestions the secretary of state may have made. It is conceivable that the stirring final passage of the speech, like the peroration of the First Inaugural, may have been suggested by Seward and refined by Lincoln.

Lifting the President's spirits was a telegram from his wife announcing that their son might be "slightly better." Upon reading that hopeful message, Lincoln remarked to the guard stationed outside his room at the Wills house: "This telegram was from home. My little boy has been very sick, but he is better."

President Lincoln arrived at the Gettysburg Railroad Station around 5 p.m. on November 18. He walked from the train station to the David Wills house, where the Willses hosted Lincoln and other dignitaries while in Gettysburg.

PRESIDENT LINCOLN STAYED THE EVENING OF WEDNESDAY, NOVEMBER 18, IN THE DAVID WILLS HOUSE,
ONE OF THE LARGEST HOMES IN TOWN, LOCATED ON THE GETTYSBURG TOWN SQUARE. WILLS WAS A PROMINENT ATTORNEY WHO
LED THE EFFORTS FOR THE DEVELOPMENT OF THE SOLDIERS' NATIONAL CEMETERY. HE INVITED LINCOLN TO SPEAK AT THE DEDICATION.

I appear before you, fellow-citizens, merely to thank you for this compliment. The inference is a very fair one that you would hear me for a little while at least, were I to commence to make a speech. I do not appear before you for the purpose of doing so, and for several substantial reasons. The most substantial of these is that I have no speech to make. [LAUGHTER.] In my position it is somewhat important that I should not say any foolish things.

A VOICE FROM THE CROWD—"IF YOU CAN HELP IT."

It very often happens that the only way to help it is to say nothing at all. [LAUGHTER.] Believing that is my present condition this evening, I must beg of you to excuse me from addressing you further.

REMARKS TO CITIZENS OF GETTYSBURG, PENNSYLVANIA, NOVEMBER 18, 1863

NEW YORK TRIBUNE, NOVEMBER 20, 1863. "AFTER SUPPER THE PRESIDENT WAS SERENADED BY THE EXCELLENT BAND OF THE 5TH NEW-YORK ARTILLERY. AFTER REPEATED CALLS, MR. LINCOLN AT LENGTH PRESENTED HIMSELF, WHEN HE WAS LOUDLY CHEERED."

ABRAHAM LINCOLN WAS AMONG THIRTY-EIGHT DINNER GUESTS AT THE WILLS HOME ON NOVEMBER 18. THE PRESIDENT WAS SERENADED INTO THE EVENING. AFTER REPEATED REQUESTS, LINCOLN BRIEFLY ADDRESSED THE CROWD GATHERED OUTSIDE.

THE BED IS ORIGINAL TO THE SECOND-FLOOR BEDROOM OF THE DAVID WILLS HOUSE, AND OTHER PIECES OF FURNITURE ARE BELIEVED TO BE ORIGINAL TO THE ROOM OR HOUSE. LINCOLN PUT THE FINISHING TOUCHES ON THE GETTYSBURG ADDRESS THE NIGHT BEFORE, AND POSSIBLY DID LAST MINUTE FINE TUNING THE MORNING OF THURSDAY, NOVEMBER 19.

DAVID AND CATHERINE WILLS HAD A COMPLETELY FULL HOUSE OF GUESTS THE EVENING OF NOVEMBER 18, AS DID ALL THE HOTELS IN GETTYSBURG. THE WILLSES ACCOMMODATED GUESTS IN EVERY ROOM OF THEIR HOME, MRS. WILLS REQUESTING PRESIDENT LINCOLN TO STAY IN HER ROOM. THE SECOND-FLOOR BEDROOM HAS WINDOWS THAT FACE THE TOWN SQUARE.

EARLY IN THE MORNING ON NOVEMBER 19, PRESIDENT LINCOLN TOURED THE BATTLEFIELD WITH SECRETARY OF STATE WILLIAM SEWARD BY CARRIAGE. THERE IS NO RECORD OF WHERE LINCOLN AND SEWARD VISITED, BUT IT IS BELIEVED THEY MAY HAVE GONE TO THE LOCATION WHERE GENERAL JOHN REYNOLDS WAS KILLED ON THE FIRST DAY'S BATTLEFIELD.

On the early morning tour of the battlefield, it is possible President Lincoln and Secretary Seward rode by General Meade's headquarters. The general's headquarters had been in a small house owned by Lydia Leister, a farmstead located directly on the Taneytown Road, very near town. Following the battle, General Meade's headquarters was always of particular interest to visitors, stereoview producers, and publications.

MOST ROADS ON THE BATTLEFIELD TODAY DID NOT EXIST IN 1863. THE LYDIA LEISTER FARM, GENERAL MEADE'S HEADQUARTERS
DURING THE BATTLE, IS ON A ROUTE MANY PEOPLE FOLLOWED TO OBSERVE THE BATTLEFIELD IN THE YEARS FOLLOWING THE BATTLE.
TWO MAIN ROADS FOLLOWED THE FULL LENGTH OF THE SECOND AND THIRD DAY'S BATTLEFIELD SOUTH OF TOWN—
THE TANEYTOWN ROAD AND THE EMMITSBURG ROAD. THE CULP'S HILL AREA HAS ALWAYS BEEN ACCESSED FROM THE BALTIMORE PIKE.

THIS STONE WALL ALONG THE MILLERSTOWN ROAD (ALSO CALLED THE WHEATFIELD ROAD TODAY) RUNS THROUGH THE BATTLEFIELD, NEAR THE WHEATFIELD. THE NORTH SIDE OF LITTLE ROUND TOP IS IN THE BACKGROUND. THE MILLERSTOWN ROAD WAS THE ONLY MAIN ROAD ON THE BATTLEFIELD SOUTH OF TOWN, CONNECTING THE TANEYTOWN ROAD AND EMMITSBURG ROAD. THIS SIX-MILE ROUTE FROM THE TOWN SQUARE PASSES AREAS OFTEN NOTED IN 1863, AND SEVERAL AREAS OF HEAVY FIGHTING, INCLUDING CEMETERY HILL, GENERAL MEADE'S HEADQUARTERS, THE ROUND TOPS, THE WHEATFIELD, THE PEACH ORCHARD, AND LEE'S FINAL ASSAULT.

THE PROCESSION TO THE DEDICATION CEREMONY
...on the occasion of the consecration of the National Cemetery at Gettysburg...

EXTEMPORANEOUS SPEECH (REPLY TO PHILADELPHIA DELEGATION), JANUARY 24, 1865

The next morning, well before dawn, all roads to Gettysburg grew clogged with wagons, buggies, horseback riders, and pedestrians eager to attend the well-publicized ceremony. Others came pouring out of the uncomfortable trains that chugged into the local station. Quickly they overflowed the town's streets. According to one reporter, most "were fathers, mothers, brothers, and sisters, who had come from distant parts to look at and weep over the remains of their fallen kindred, or to gather up the honored relics and bear them back to the burial grounds of their native homes – in relating what they had suffered and endured, and what part their loved ones had borne in the memorable days of July." An elderly Massachusetts gentleman remarked, "I have a son who fell in the first day's fight, and I have come to take back his body, for his mother's heart is breaking, and she will not be satisfied till it is brought home to her." A Pennsylvanian explained: "My brother was killed in the charge of the Pennsylvania Reserves on the enemy when they were driven from Little Round-top, but we don't know where his remains are."

The sky, at first overcast, cleared during the ceremony. John Hay called it "one of the most beautiful Indian Summer days ever enjoyed." As people swarmed into town, Lincoln rose early, toured the battlefield with Seward, and polished his address. To a reporter who had managed to gain access to the Wills house, the President said: "The best course for the journals of the country to pursue, if they wished to sustain the Government, was to stand by the officers of the army." Rather than harping on military failures, newspapers should urge people to render "all the aid in their power" to the war effort. At 10 o'clock he joined the procession to the cemetery, led by his friend Ward Hill Lamon, the marshal in charge of arrangements. Upon emerging from the Wills house wearing a black suit and white gauntlets, Lincoln encountered a huge crowd which greeted him with "enthusiastic and long continued cheers," causing him to blush. A newspaper in nearby Chambersburg reported that before the procession got underway, "many persons gathered around the President, shaking him by the hand. He received every one in the most gracious manner. One of our own well known citizens accosted him with 'How are you father Abraham?' following it quickly with the remark, 'I am most happy to meet you, Mr. President!'" Lincoln "received the salutation becomingly and gave his special interrogator one of his best bows." His admirers insisted on shaking hands until the marshals finally intervened to protect his arm from more wrenching.

A journalist noted that Lincoln's "awkwardness which is so often remarked does not extend to his

FOLLOWING THE TOUR OF THE BATTLEFIELD, PRESIDENT LINCOLN RETURNED TO THE DAVID WILLS HOUSE TO PREPARE FOR THE PROCESSION TO THE DEDICATION CEREMONY. AT AROUND 10:00 A.M., LINCOLN EXITED THE WILLS HOUSE AND WAS GREETED WITH CHEERS FROM THE CROWD. HE MOUNTED A HORSE AND THE PROCESSION TO THE SOLDIERS' NATIONAL CEMETERY BEGAN.

The first hint of light accentuates the Evergreen Cemetery Gatehouse as the sun rises above the horizon on a crisp autumn morning. The Gatehouse was near the center of activity on Thursday, November 19. The dedication procession began at the Gettysburg town square, proceeding to the Soldiers' National Cemetery one mile away, directly next to Evergreen Cemetery (the town of Gettysburg's cemetery).

The sun never broke to life and warmth on a fairer fall day than this. A sharp night's frost was succeeded by one of the most beautiful Indian Summer days ever enjoyed. At an early hour, long before sunrise, the roads leading to Gettysburg were crowded by citizens from every quarter thronging into the village in every kind of vehicle—old Pennsylvania wagons, spring wagons, carts, family carriages, buggies, and more fashionable modern vehicles, all crowded with citizens—kept pouring into the town in one continual string, while the roads were constantly dotted with pedestrians by twos, by threes, singly, and in companies, all facing towards the village.

Thus the thronging in continued until late in the day, while the railroad disgorged its eager crowds, while the streets, ever filling, overflowed with the invading host.

Soon after breakfast I rode out to the Cemetery, and the crowds that I left in the town seemed to have duplicated themselves, and to have scattered all over the extensive area of the battle ground, wandering out to the seminary, strolling about the college, laboring to the summit of Round Top, examining Culp's Hill, tracing the plan of the Cemetery, seeking relics everywhere: the whole landscape was fairly studded with visitors, mostly on foot, many on horseback, and not a few in carriages, and, with maps in hand, getting up the field of battle, and realizing for the first time the grandeur and extent of the struggle about which they had heard so much.

Returning to the village, the scattered concourse we had left miles out in the country seemed to have got there before us, for the streets were full to overflowing, and yet they came.

The town was now enlivened by the procession forming and by the marshals and military. The various orders and delegations were being placed and arranged in the procession ready to set out.

At about 10 the President issued from Mr. Wills' house, and was greeted with three hearty cheers. Soon someone proclaimed three cheers for Father Abraham, and they were given with a will. Another call for three cheers for the next President of the United States was responded to with no less enthusiasm.

In the meanwhile the President had mounted, and was besieged by an eager crowd thronging around him, and anxious for the pleasure of taking him by the hand, while he sat pleasantly enjoying the hearty welcome thus spontaneously accorded, until the marshals, having mercy upon his oft-wrung arm and wearying exertions, caused the crowd to desist and allow the President to sit in peace upon his horse. But the people, not yet satisfied, must have another three cheers for honest Old Abe, and they fairly eclipsed all the others.

Mr. Lincoln appeared in black, with the usual crape bound around his hat in memory of his little son, and with white gauntlets upon his hands. The list of notables who were present is given in another column, and many of them mounted when he did, and they remained conversing together waiting for the moving of the procession.

Mr. Lincoln remarked upon the fair prospects spread out before him, and observed that he had expected to see more woods, an expectation, doubtless, that had been entertained by many besides himself.

In the meanwhile the throng of swaying, eager people, more remote from him, were crowding and jostling, ever restlessly trying to get a glimpse of Mr. Lincoln, many of whom, doubtless, saw for the first time a live President of the United States.

When the procession began to move I hastened to the platform, and arrived there long before the cavalcade appeared upon the ground. Taking our seat among the reporters, we endeavored to prepare ourselves to enable the readers of THE CHRONICLE to obtain some idea of the day's proceedings.

John Hay, President Lincoln's Assistant Personal Secretary and part-time correspondent, Washington <u>Daily Morning Chronicle</u>, November 21, 1863 horsemanship." Other reporters wrote that once he had mounted "a splendid black horse," Lincoln "sat up the tallest and grandest rider in the procession, bowing and nearly laughing his acknowledgments to the oft-repeated cheers – 'Hurrah for Old Abe;' and 'We're coming, Father Abraham,' and one solitary greeting of its kind, 'God save Abraham Lincoln.'" In a letter written by a Gettysburg resident ten days after the event, the President was described as "gracefully bowing with a modest smile and uncovered head to the throng of women, men and children that greeted him from the doors and windows." The writer added that even though Lincoln appeared "cheerful and happy on that day an observant eye could see that the dreadful responsibility that this nation and this wicked rebellion has cast upon him has had its marked effect, and that he feels the terrible responsibility that rests upon him."

Commissioner of Public Buildings Benjamin Brown French, acting as an assistant to the master of ceremonies (Lincoln's good friend Ward Hill Lamon), was struck by the way that the citizenry lionized the President. "Abraham Lincoln is the idol of the American people at this moment," French confided to his journal. "Anyone who saw & heard as I did, the hurricane of applause that met his every movement at Gettysburg would know that he lived in every heart. It was no cold, faint, shadow of a kind reception – it was a tumultuous outpouring of exultation, from true and loving hearts, at the sight of a man whom everyone knew to be honest and true and sincere in every act of his life, and every pulsation of his heart. It was the spontaneous outburst of heartfelt confidence in their own President." A Virginia woman visiting Gettysburg recorded in her diary that "[s]uch homage I never saw or imagined could be shown to any one person as the people bestow on Lincoln. The very mention of his name brings forth shouts of applause."

Amid the firing of minute guns and the huzzahing of the crowd, the procession, according to John Hay, "formed itself in an orphanly sort of way & moved out with very little help from anybody." Led by the Marine Band, the line of marchers and riders advanced slowly, reaching the cemetery in about twenty minutes. Thanks to recent rains, the cavalcade stirred up little dust. A Gettysburg resident described the procession as "a grand and impressive sight. I have no language to depict it and though the mighty mass rolled on as the waves of the ocean, everything was in perfect order."

The procession including President Lincoln riding horseback, dignitaries, and the U.S. military, all led by the Marine Band, started at the town square and headed south, passing the William Walker house at 256 Baltimore Street. Many people went ahead of the procession to the Soldiers' National Cemetery to find spots as close as possible to the platform in order to hear the several speakers and music.

Many of the homes on Baltimore Street appear much like they did in 1863, and though many things have changed in 150 years, Baltimore Street and all of Gettysburg have preserved a timeless character.

This Civil War building has had a later addition like many buildings from 1863, but maintains an enduring quality. It was the Methodist parsonage in 1863. It has a cannon ball stuck in the wall on the second floor, one of at least a dozen homes in town sharing a similar story. In almost all the structures, the cannon balls were placed in the walls after they were repaired, because the cannon balls almost always smashed through the walls after striking them.

THE GEORGE AND HETTIE SHRIVER HOUSE AT 309 BALTIMORE STREET IS NOW THE SHRIVER HOUSE MUSEUM.
GEORGE SHRIVER WAS DEDICATED TO THE UNION AND HAD VOLUNTEERED FOR SERVICE IN AUGUST, 1861, AND MUSTERED
INTO A CAVALRY UNIT IN MARYLAND. TWO YEARS LATER WHEN LEE'S ARMY INVADED HIS HOMETOWN, HE WAS UNABLE TO
BE THERE WHEN THE CONFEDERATES COMPLETELY RANSACKED HIS HOME. HETTIE AND THEIR TWO DAUGHTERS FLED FOR
SAFETY AND LATER RETURNED TO A DEVASTATED HOME AND TOWN. EVEN WORSE, GEORGE SHRIVER WAS CAPTURED IN
ACTION, AND SENT TO THE NOTORIOUS ANDERSONVILLE PRISON IN GEORGIA WHERE ALMOST 13,000 UNION SOLDIERS DIED.

James and Margaret Pierce were close friends and neighbors of the Shriver family. The Pierce house is now the Tillie Pierce House Inn at 301 Baltimore Street, named after their daughter Matilda J. "Tillie" Pierce. Tillie was a fifteen-year-old girl during the battle and she later wrote a vivid account about her experiences during and after the battle. She had left town for safety with Hettie Shriver and her daughters to seek shelter at Hettie's family farm located near the Round Tops, only to find themselves completely engulfed in war. Tillie and the Shrivers helped with wounded and dying soldiers for several days before coming home to a town forever changed.

The Tyson Brothers (Charles & Isaac) made at least three photographs looking straight north up Baltimore Street on Thursday, November 19, 1863. This image was made a short time before the procession to the dedication started coming down the hill from the town square. Note the white carriage on the right side of the street, with American flags on each side and drawn by white horses. (Adams County Historical Society collection)

In this dramatic photograph made by Charles & Isaac Tyson of the procession on Baltimore Street, the column of soldiers is clearly visible at the saddle in the street next to present-day Alumni Park. The procession was led by the Marine Band in the one-mile parade to the Soldiers' National Cemetery. President Lincoln may be in one of the Tyson Brother's photographs, but he certainly cannot be identified. (National Archives and Records Administration collection)

Detail of photograph from previous page (image made by Charles & Isaac Tyson)

The John Rupp house is on the left (the current Rupp House, home to the Gettysburg Foundation, was built in 1868); and the John Winebrenner house shown on page 100, is the third house down on the right. There are three sycamore trees on the right side of the street. All three trees are hard to distinguish in the photograph because the three were planted lined up exactly north and south. All three were there until 2005 when one of the twin sycamores in front of the Winebrenner house had to be taken down. At least four bullets were found lodged in the tree. Tree rings determined the tree to be 180 years old in 2005—38 years old when Lincoln rode by. The two giant sycamores there today were probably planted at the same time, in 1825.

This photograph reveals that many leaves can clearly be seen on the sycamores, while other trees are bare. (National Archives and Records Administration collection)

ORDER OF PROCESSION

FOR THE

INAUGURATION

OF THE

National Cemetery at Gettysburg, Pa.

ON THE 19TH NOVEMBER, 1863.

Military, under command of Major-General COUCH.
Major-General MEADE and Staff, and the officers and soldiers of the Army of the Potomac.
Officers of the Navy and Marine Corps of the United States.
Aids.   CHIEF MARSHAL.   Aids.
PRESIDENT OF THE UNITED STATES.
Members of the Cabinet.
Assistant Secretaries of the Several Executive Departments.
General-in-Chief of the Army, and Staff.
Lieutenant-General SCOTT and Rear-Admiral STEWART.
Judges of the U. S. Supreme Court.
Hon. EDWARD EVERETT, Orator of the day, and the Chaplain.
Governors of the States, and their Staffs.
Commissioners of the States on the Inauguration of the Cemetery.
Bearers with the Flags of the States.
VICE-PRESIDENT OF THE UNITED STATES and Speaker of the House of Representatives.
Members of the two Houses of Congress.
Officers of the two Houses of Congress.
Mayors of Cities.
Gettysburg Committee of Arrangements.
Officers and members of the United States Sanitary Commission.
Committees of Different Religious Bodies.
U. S. Military Telegraphic Corps.
Officers and Representatives of Adams Express Company.
Officers of different Telegraph Companies.
Hospital Corps of the Army.
Soldiers' Relief Associations.
Knights Templar.
Masonic Fraternity.
Independent Order of Odd-Fellows.
Other Benevolent Associations.
Literary, Scientific, and Industrial Associations.
The Press.
Officers and members of Loyal Leagues.
Fire Companies.
Citizens of the State of Pennsylvania.
Citizens of other States.
Citizens of the District of Columbia.
Citizens of the several Territories.

Programme of Arrangements and Order of Exercises

FOR THE INAUGURATION

OF THE

NATIONAL CEMETERY AT GETTYSBURG,

ON THE 19TH OF NOVEMBER, 1863.

The military will form in Gettysburg at 9 o'clock a. m., on Carlisle street, north of the square, its right resting on the square, opposite McClellan's Hotel, under the direction of Major General Couch.

The State Marshals and Chief Marshal's aids will assemble in the public square at the same hour.

All civic bodies except the citizens of States will assemble, according to the foregoing printed programme, on York street at the same hour.

The delegation of Pennsylvania citizens will form on Chambersburg street, its right resting on the square, and the other citizen delegations, in their order, will form on the same street in rear of the Pennsylvania delegation.

The Marshals of the States are charged with the duty of forming their several delegations so that they will assume their appropriate positions when the main procession moves.

The head of the column will move at precisely 10 o'clock a. m.

The route will be up Baltimore street to the Emmittsburg road; thence to the junction of the Taneytown road; thence, by the latter road, to the Cemetery, where the military will form in line, as the General in command may order, for the purpose of saluting the President of the United States.

The military will then close up, and occupy the space on the left of the stand.

The civic procession will advance and occupy the area in front of the stand, the military leaving sufficient space between them and the line of graves for the civic procession to pass.

The ladies will occupy the right of the stand, and it is desirable that they be upon the ground as early as ten o'clock a. m.

The exercises will take place as soon as the military and civic bodies are in position, as follows:

Music.
Prayer.
Music.
ORATION.
Music.
DEDICATORY REMARKS BY THE PRESIDENT OF THE UNITED STATES.
Dirge.
Benediction.

After the benediction the procession will be dismissed, and the State Marshals and special aids to the Chief Marshal will form on Baltimore street, and return to the Court-house in Gettysburg, where a meeting of the marshals will be held.

An appropriate salute will be fired in Gettysburg on the day of the celebration, under the direction of Maj. Gen. Couch.

WARD H. LAMON,
Marshal-in-Chief.

Gideon & Pearson, Printers, 511 Ninth st., Washington.

THIS IS AN ORIGINAL PROGRAM FOR THE PROCESSION AND DEDICATION OF THE SOLDIERS' NATIONAL CEMETERY, REFERRED TO AS THE NATIONAL CEMETERY AT GETTYSBURG ON THE PROGRAM AND IN MANY PUBLICATIONS. (GETTYSBURG NATIONAL MILITARY PARK MUSEUM COLLECTION)

ABOVE: THE CONFEDERATES CONTROLLED MOST OF GETTYSBURG ON JULY 2 AND 3, CREATING A FIERCE SKIRMISH LINE ON THE SOUTH EDGE OF TOWN. THEY OCCUPIED THE JOHN WINEBRENNER HOUSE AND MANY OTHERS DURING THE BATTLE. NUMEROUS BULLET HOLES CAN BE SEEN ON THE SOUTH SIDE OF THIS HOUSE IN THE BRICK AND SHUTTERS, MOST THANKS TO UNION SHARPSHOOTERS ON CEMETERY HILL. THE WINEBRENNER HOUSE HAD TWIN SYCAMORE TREES ALONG BALTIMORE STREET DURING THE BATTLE, AND SEVERAL MONTHS LATER WHEN PRESIDENT LINCOLN AND THE PROCESSION TO THE DEDICATION PASSED UNDER THEIR BRANCHES. THIS HUGE WITNESS TO HISTORY THAT STILL STANDS TODAY IS AT LEAST 180 YEARS OLD.

FOLLOWING PAGE: ONE OF THE ORIGINAL THREE SYCAMORE TREES, THIS GIANT SYCAMORE STANDS IN ALUMNI PARK ON BALTIMORE STREET, DIRECTLY NEXT TO THE WINEBRENNER HOUSE. THIS IMAGE WAS MADE ON NOVEMBER 18 WITH THE TREE FULL OF AUTUMN LEAVES. THE TREE AT THE WINEBRENNER HOUSE HAD TURNED COLOR TWO WEEKS EARLIER.

THE DEDICATION OF THE SOLDIERS' NATIONAL CEMETERY

I would like to speak in terms of praise due to the many brave officers and soldiers who have fought in the cause of the Union and liberties of the country from the beginning of the war.

EXTEMPORANEOUS SPEECH AT THE EXECUTIVE MANSION, JULY 7, 1863

At the cemetery, Lincoln and three dozen other honored guests – including governors, congressmen, senators, cabinet members, and generals – took their places on the 12' x 20' platform. As the President slowly approached that stage, the 15,000 spectators maintained a respectful silence. In keeping with the solemnity of the occasion, men removed their hats. As the President sat waiting for the ceremony to begin, Martin D. Potter of the Cincinnati <u>Commercial</u> sketched a pen portrait of him: "A Scotch type of countenance, you say, with the disadvantage of emaciation by a siege of Western ague. It is a thoughtful, kindly, care-worn face, impressive in repose, the eyes cast down, the lids thin and firmly set, the cheeks sunken, and the whole indicating weariness, and anything but good health."

(Around that time a White House caller thought Lincoln was so weary that he resembled "a New York omnibus beast at night who had been driven all day" during an August heat spell. Journalists reported that he was "not looking well," that he was "careworn," that he appeared "thin and feeble," and that "his eyes have lost their humorous expression." Lincoln refused to heed the advice of friends who urged him to leave the capital to recruit his health. In fact, he may have been suffering from the attack of smallpox that would leave him bedridden for ten days once he arrived back in Washington.)

Once the other dignitaries were seated, a dirge opened the proceedings, followed by the Rev. Dr. Thomas H. Stockton's long prayer which, Hay quipped, "thought it was an oration." Stockton may have bored Hay but he brought tears to many eyes, including those of the President. For the next two hours, Everett delivered his polished, carefully researched and memorized speech describing the battle, analyzing the causes and nature of the war, rebutting secessionist arguments, predicting a quick postwar sectional reconciliation, citing ancient Greek funeral rites, and denouncing the enemy. Lincoln, who was "visibly pleased with the oration," occasionally smiled at especially apt passages. At one point, he whispered his approval in Seward's ear and at another he slapped the thigh of the secretary of state. When Everett alluded to the suffering of the dying troops, tears came to Lincoln's eyes, as they did to the eyes of most auditors. After Everett finished, Lincoln shook his hand and said: "I am more than gratified, I am grateful to you."

After a musical interlude, Lincoln slowly rose to speak, causing a stir of expectation. His "reception was

JOHN HAY DESCRIBED THAT NOVEMBER DAY AS "ONE OF THE MOST BEAUTIFUL INDIAN SUMMER DAYS EVER ENJOYED".
THE EVERGREEN CEMETERY GATEHOUSE HAS BECOME A SYMBOLIC REMINDER OF THE GETTYSBURG ADDRESS.
THE EXACT SPOT OF THE PLATFORM WHERE ABRAHAM LINCOLN DELIVERED THE GETTYSBURG ADDRESS IS UNKNOWN, BUT
IT WAS BETWEEN 170 AND 200 YARDS FROM THE GATEHOUSE IN WHAT IS NOW THE EVERGREEN CEMETERY. THE GATEHOUSE
WAS THE ONLY STRUCTURE THAT COULD BE SEEN ON THE LANDSCAPE FOR A LONG DISTANCE ON THE DAY OF THE DEDICATION.

quite cordial," noted Ben: Perley Poore of the Boston Journal. John Hay reported that when Lamon introduced Lincoln, the President was "vociferously cheered by the vast audience." As spectators on the outer fringes of the crowd pressed forward, those closer to the platform pushed back, causing a brief disturbance. A nurse in the audience recalled that she and the others "seemed like fishes in a barrel," so tightly jammed together that they "almost suffocated." When calm was restored, the President put on his glasses, drew a paper from his pocket, and "in a sharp, unmusical, and treble voice," read his brief remarks "in a very deliberate manner, with strong emphasis, and with a most business-like air." His "clear, loud" voice "could be distinctly heard at the extreme limits of the large assemblage." John Hay recorded in his diary that Lincoln spoke "in a firm free way, with more grace than is his wont." In his journalistic account of the event, Hay wrote that as Lincoln spoke, he "sensibly felt the solemnity of the occasion, and controlled himself by an effort."

Lincoln's words were taken down by reporters whose accounts differ slightly. The Associated Press correspondent, Joseph L. Gilbert, claimed that after delivering the speech, Lincoln allowed him to copy the text from his manuscript. Charles Hale of the Boston Daily Advertiser took down Lincoln's words in shorthand. Conflating these two versions, we can obtain a good idea of what Lincoln actually said. It differs from the revised versions he made later when donating copies to charitable causes. The following text is what he probably said, with bracketed italics representing revisions he made for the final version (the so-called "Bliss copy" of the speech): "Four score and seven years ago our fathers brought forth upon [on] this continent a new nation, conceived in liberty, and dedicated to the proposition that all men are created equal. [Applause.] Now we are engaged in a great civil war, testing whether that nation or any nation so conceived and so dedicated, can long endure. We are met on a great battle-field of that war. We are met [have come] to dedicate a portion of it [that field] as the [a] final resting place of [for] those who here gave their lives that that nation might live. It is altogether fitting and proper that we should do this. But, in a larger sense, we cannot dedicate, we cannot consecrate, we cannot hallow this ground. The brave men, living and dead, who struggled here have consecrated it far above our poor power to add or detract. [Applause.] The world will little note nor long remember what we say here, but it can never forget what they did here. [Applause.] It is for us, the living, rather to be dedicated here to the unfinished work that [which] they [who fought here] have thus far so nobly carried on [advanced]. [Applause.] It is rather for us to be here dedicated to the great task remaining before us, that from these honored dead we take increased devotion to that cause for which they here gave [they gave] the last full measure of devotion; that we here highly resolve that these dead shall not have died in vain [applause]; that the nation shall, under God, [nation, under God, shall] have a new birth of freedom; and that Government of the people, by the people, [for the people] and for the people, shall not perish from the earth. [Long-continued applause.]"

THIS PHOTOGRAPH WAS MADE BY PETER S. WEAVER ON NOVEMBER 19, 1863—ONE OF TWO HIGH-ANGLE IMAGES KNOWN TO EXIST FROM THE EVENT, BOTH BY WEAVER. THIS PHOTOGRAPH WAS MADE FROM A WINDOW ON THE SECOND FLOOR OF THE EVERGREEN CEMETERY GATEHOUSE FACING WEST. THE FLAGPOLE CAN BE SEEN NEAR THE CENTER AND THE GROUP ON THE SPEAKER'S PLATFORM IS ON THE LEFT, BETWEEN 170 AND 200 YARDS AWAY. THE PHOTOGRAPH ON PAGE 108 IS TAKEN FROM ALMOST 180 DEGREES, ON THE OPPOSITE SIDE OF THE CEREMONY—THE WINDOW IN THE GATEHOUSE USED TO MAKE THIS IMAGE CAN BE SEEN OPEN. (LIBRARY OF CONGRESS COLLECTION)

AT ABOUT 11:20, THE PRESIDENT ARRIVED UPON THE PLATFORM, ACCOMPANIED BY SECRETARIES SEWARD, BLAIR, AND USHER. SOON GOVERNOR TOD AND GOVERNOR BROUGH CAME NEAR, AND MR. TOD, IN A HEARTY, CORDIAL MANNER, SAID: "MR. PRESIDENT, I WANT YOU TO SHAKE HANDS WITH ME;" AND MR. LINCOLN AS CORDIALLY RESPONDED. HE THEN INTRODUCED GOVERNOR BROUGH TO THE PRESIDENT, AND ALSO TO MR. SEWARD, WHO SAID, "WHY, I HAVE JUST SEEN GOVERNOR DENNISON, OF OHIO, AND HERE ARE TWO MORE GOVERNORS OF OHIO—HOW MANY MORE GOVERNORS HAS OHIO?" "SHE HAS ONLY ONE MORE, SIR," SAID GOVERNOR BROUGH, "AND HE'S ACROSS THE WATER."

BY-AND-BY, GOVERNOR TOD SAID HE HAD CALLED ON GOVERNOR SEWARD, BUT HAD NOT FOUND HIM AT HOME; ALSO, ON MR. USHER: "YES, SIR," SAID SEWARD, "I VISITED THE GROUND AROUND THE SEMINARY THIS MORNING, AND MR. LINCOLN JOINED IN. WELL, GOVERNOR, YOU SEEM TO HAVE BEEN TO THE STATE DEPARTMENT AND TO THE INTERIOR, I WILL NOW GO WITH YOU TO THE POST OFFICE DEPARTMENT;" WHEREUPON HE TURNED TO SECRETARY BLAIR AND INTRODUCED GOVERNORS BROUGH AND TOD TO HIM.

THE CROWD UPON THE GROUND WERE KEPT IN THE FORM OF A HOLLOW SQUARE, WITHIN WHICH, WHILE THESE THINGS WERE PROCEEDING, THE PROCESSION HAD FILED AND THE VARIOUS COMPANIES FORMING IT HAD TAKEN UP A POSITION AROUND THE PLATFORM, WHILE THOSE WHO HAD TICKETS TOOK THEIR SEATS UPON IT.

WE NOTICED DELEGATIONS FROM BALTIMORE, WASHINGTON, AND PHILADELPHIA, AND FROM THE MASONS, ODD-FELLOWS, TEMPLARS, AND MANY OF THE SONS OF MALTA, WHO WERE NOT IN REGALIA. THE SANITARY COMMISSION, TOO, WERE THERE, CONSPICUOUS BY THEIR BANNER, AND PRECIOUS BY THE MEMORY OF THEIR EXTENDED USEFULNESS AND VALUABLE SERVICES. MANY STATES, TOO, WERE REPRESENTED, AND FLAGS AND BANNERS ENLIVENED THE SCENE.

FIVE OR SIX BANDS WERE ALSO PRESENT, AMONG WHICH WERE THE MARINE BAND, OF WASHINGTON, BIRGFELD'S BAND, THE BAND OF THE 2D REGULARS, FROM FORT MCHENRY, NEW YORK REGIMENTAL BAND, AND OTHERS.

AT TWENTY MINUTES TO TWELVE, HON. EDWARD EVERETT ARRIVED, AND AFTER BEING INTRODUCED TO THE PRESIDENT, THE EXERCISES AT ONCE PROCEEDED. MARSHAL LAMON FIRST ANNOUNCED THAT A LETTER HAD JUST BEEN RECEIVED FROM GENERAL SCOTT, REGRETTING THAT HIS INCREASING INFIRMITIES RENDERED HIM UNABLE TO BE PRESENT UPON THE OCCASION.

BIRGFELD'S BAND THEN PLAYED AN INTRODUCTORY DIRGE, SOLEMN AND SUITABLE FOR THE OCCASION. THE REV. THOMAS H. STOCKTON THEN OFFERED A VERY IMPRESSIVE PRAYER. THIS WAS FOLLOWED BY BIRGFELD'S BAND, WHO GAVE US THE OLD HUNDRED IN ALL ITS GRAND AND SUBLIME BEAUTY—AFTER WHICH THE HON. EDWARD EVERETT WAS INTRODUCED BY MARSHAL LAMON. SOME IDIOT IN THE CROWD AT ONCE PROPOSED THREE CHEERS FOR EVERETT, WHICH THE GOOD SENSE OF THE PEOPLE IMMEDIATELY DECIDED SO IRREVERENT UPON SUCH AN OCCASION THAT NO ONE RESPONDED, AND MR. IDIOT SUBSIDED.

AT THIS TIME THE COUP D'OEIL OF THE SCENE WAS TRULY GRAND. CROWDS OF CITIZENS SURROUNDED THE STAND AND STRETCHED AWAY INTO THE DISTANCE, FAR OUT OF ANY POSSIBLE RANGE OF HEARING. MANY WERE IN MOURNING, AND THE UPTURNED TEARFUL EYES OF THOSE WHO WERE NEAR, INDICATED TOO PLAINLY THAT TO THEM THE DEDICATION WAS A SAD PILGRIMAGE ALSO. MILITARY OFFICERS AND MARSHALS ON HORSEBACK, SCATTERED THROUGH THE CROWD, ADDED A PLEASING VARIETY TO THE SCENE; WHILE THE VARIOUS REGIMENTAL BANDS, SOCIETIES IN THEIR REGALIA, AND THE BRIGHT AND GAY UNIFORMS OF OFFICERS AND MARSHALS, THE BANNERS, FLAGS, AND DEVICES OF THE VARIOUS REGIMENTS, ASSOCIATIONS, AND DELEGATIONS, ALL CONTRIBUTED TO PRODUCE A BLENDING AND CONTRAST OF COLORS HIGHLY PLEASING TO BEHOLD.

Around, far off, scattered over the landscape, were crowds of people who, despairing of a near approach to the stand, the centre of interest, were satisfying their curiosity and enjoying the scene apparently apart from it. Below lay Gettysburg, deserted and flag-bedecked, behind it the seminary and college, with their clustering historical associations; stretching before and beyond was the beautiful battlefield, now giving rich promise, as it had yielded past evidence of its abundant fertility. On the one side Culp's Hill, now precious in history, and on the other, far back in the distance, and surmounted by our beautiful flag, was the victory-crowned summit of Round Top. Far, far off, in distinct outline, were the South Mountains, forming a well defined frame to the whole picture. Minute guns added their impressiveness to the scene, while a daguerreotypist, with his instrument prominently placed at the outskirts of the main crowd, by the aid of the softly-glowing, hazy sun, endeavors to snatch and forever preserve the animated foreground, rich in eminent citizens.

Prominent in that foreground must not be omitted a beautiful in memoriam banner, born by a delegation of the Army of the Potomac, from the hospital at York, of which they, who had been wounded at Gettysburg, were yet inmates. This banner was in the deepest mourning. Upon it was an urn and an inscription: "Honor to our brave comrades." Upon the other side was, "In memory of those who fell at Gettysburg, July 1st, 2d, and 3d, 1863."

Mr. Everett spoke for about two hours, and his oration, fully reported elsewhere, need not be here produced. Those who read it will find that he did ample justice to his former celebrity, and to the impressive occasion.

After the oration the Baltimore Union Glee Club sung in a very beautiful style. A poem, by B. B. French, inspired and written upon the battlefield, was then delivered . . . .

. . . The President then delivered his address, which, though short, glittered with gems, evincing the gentleness and goodness of heart peculiar to him, and will receive the attention and command the admiration of all of the tens of thousands who will read it.

It seemed to us that the President sensibly felt the solemnity of the occasion, and controlled himself by an effort. This might have been fancy, but it was our impression; and as such we record it.

The brief address of the President was followed by the dirge selected for the occasion—one of Percival's—sung by a choir mainly composed of Gettysburg ladies, and accompanied by Birgfeld's band.

After this, a benediction was pronounced by Rev. Dr. —— —, the President, we believe, of the College. Marshal Lamon then announced that at half-past four the Hon. Chas. Anderson, Lieutenant Governor elect of Ohio, would deliver an address at the Presbyterian church, which the President, his Cabinet, and the people, were invited to attend; he then proclaimed the assemblage dismissed, and while the procession was reforming, a battery of the 5th regulars fired a salvo of eight rounds from their four guns.

The Marine Band, of Washington, escorted the procession back to the town, and afterwards, with other bands alternating, kept the air resonant with melody until sunset.

John Hay, President Lincoln's Assistant Personal Secretary and part-time correspondent, Washington Daily Morning Chronicle, November 21, 1863

THIS PHOTOGRAPH IS THIRD IN A SERIES OF AT LEAST THREE SURVIVING PHOTOGRAPHS, THIS IMAGE MADE A LITTLE LATER THAN THE FIRST TWO. IT IS VERY LIKELY PRESIDENT LINCOLN IS IN ONE, OR ALL THREE OF THESE IMAGES BY ALEXANDER GARDNER, BUT LINCOLN CANNOT BE IDENTIFIED FOR CERTAIN. NOTE HOW THE UNION SOLDIERS HAVE STACKED THEIR RIFLES. THE FLAGPOLE IS BELIEVED TO BE THE EXACT SPOT, OR VERY NEAR, WHERE THE SOLDIERS' NATIONAL MONUMENT STANDS TODAY.
(LIBRARY OF CONGRESS COLLECTION)

PAGES 111 & 112: THIS PHOTOGRAPH WAS MADE BY DAVID BACHRACH, JR. ON NOVEMBER 19, 1863,
OF THE DEDICATION CEREMONY FOR THE SOLDIERS' NATIONAL CEMETERY, REFERRED TO FREQUENTLY IN 1863
AS THE CONSECRATION OF THE NATIONAL CEMETERY AT GETTYSBURG. THIS IS THE ONLY KNOWN PHOTOGRAPH
WHERE PRESIDENT LINCOLN IS CLEARLY IDENTIFIABLE AT THE DEDICATION OR AT ANY PLACE WHILE IN GETTYSBURG. THE
ORIGINAL GLASS PLATE AT THE NATIONAL ARCHIVES WAS CRACKED. THIS IMAGE IS FROM A PRINT PROBABLY MADE FROM THE
ORIGINAL PLATE BEFORE IT WAS CRACKED MANY YEARS AGO. THIS IS THE ONLY KNOWN SURVIVING PHOTOGRAPH BY BACHRACH.
(NATIONAL ARCHIVES AND RECORDS ADMINISTRATION COLLECTION)

PAGES 113 & 114: THE BACHRACH PHOTOGRAPH, LIKE MANY OF THE PHOTOGRAPHS OF THE CIVIL WAR ERA, WAS
MADE WITH A CAMERA THAT USES LARGE GLASS PLATES CREATING A VERY HIGH RESOLUTION IMAGE. THIS CROPPED VERSION
OF THE PREVIOUS COMPOSITION GIVES A COMPLETELY DIFFERENT PERSPECTIVE OF THE SAME MOMENT. THE UNION SOLDIERS
PROUDLY POSING ON THE LEFT WITH MARSHALS AND MARSHAL'S AIDES IN THE CEREMONY (THE MEN WITH SASHES) ON THE RIGHT.
THE TENT BEHIND THE SPEAKER'S PLATFORM WAS ERECTED FOR EDWARD EVERETT, THE MAIN ORATOR FOR THE EVENT. PRESIDENT
LINCOLN IS FRONT AND CENTER ON THE PLATFORM BUILT TO ELEVATE DIGNITARIES AND PARTICIPANTS OF THE CEREMONY.
(NATIONAL ARCHIVES AND RECORDS ADMINISTRATION COLLECTION)

ABOVE: THIS DETAIL OF THE BACHRACH PHOTOGRAPH INCLUDES PRESIDENT LINCOLN, DIGNITARIES, JOURNALISTS,
AND PROBABLY MARSHALS AND THEIR AIDES. PRESIDENT LINCOLN CAN BE SEEN LEFT OF CENTER, HIS FEATURES CLEARLY
IDENTIFIABLE, AND ALMOST EVERYONE IS LOOKING AT HIM. HIS HEAD IS BLURRED BECAUSE HE MOVED DURING THE
LONG EXPOSURE. EXPOSURE TIMES VARIED DEPENDING ON SEVERAL FACTORS, BUT SIX TO SEVEN SECONDS WAS COMMON
WITH WET-PLATE CAMERAS. IT IS BELIEVED THIS PHOTOGRAPH WAS MADE NEAR THE BEGINNING OF THE CEREMONY.
MANY OF THE MEN SURROUNDING LINCOLN CAN ALSO BE IDENTIFIED.
(NATIONAL ARCHIVES AND RECORDS ADMINISTRATION COLLECTION)

This photograph was made by Peter S. Weaver on November 19 from the back of the William Duttera house on the Emmitsburg Road, looking east toward the crest of Cemetery Hill. The flagpole and a large crowd surrounding the ceremony can be seen on the horizon, with the gatehouse the only structure in sight. This was one of the areas for carriages and wagons. The Taneytown Road is lined by stone walls and can be seen in the center of the photograph. As with the images by Alexander Gardner, a light breeze out of the south is apparent. Note the broad, rounded crest of Cemetery Hill which looks much different at the national cemetery today. (Hanover Area Historical Society collection)

The Soldiers' National Monument has mistakenly been described as the site of the platform where Abraham Lincoln delivered the Gettysburg Address. The actual site is a hundred yards or less away in the Evergreen Cemetery, but the exact spot is unknown. The monument is the central point of the Soldiers' National Cemetery, and it stands at the crest of Cemetery Hill, directly along the location of the Union line during the battle.

THE SOLDIERS' NATIONAL MONUMENT IN THE NATIONAL CEMETERY IS A MEMORIAL DEDICATED TO ALL
UNION SOLDIERS WHO DIED AT GETTYSBURG. CONSTRUCTION BEGAN SOON AFTER THE WAR ENDED IN 1865.
AN INSCRIPTION ON THE MONUMENT INCLUDES THE LAST FOUR LINES OF THE GETTYSBURG ADDRESS.
IT STANDS AT OR NEAR THE SPOT WHERE THE FLAGPOLE WAS ERECTED FOR THE DEDICATION CEREMONY.

THE TWILIGHT OF DUSK COMES TO THE END OF A BEAUTIFUL AUTUMN DAY AT THE SOLDIERS' NATIONAL CEMETERY. 3557 UNION SOLDIERS ARE BURIED HERE. SEVEN CONFIRMED CONFEDERATE SOLDIERS ARE BURIED HERE (THOUGH NINE IS PROBABLY MORE ACCURATE) WHO WERE MISTAKENLY IDENTIFIED AS FEDERAL TROOPS. IN THE 1870s, EFFORTS BY SOUTHERN VETERANS' SOCIETIES EVENTUALLY RELOCATED 3,200 CONFEDERATE REMAINS FROM THE BATTLEFIELD GRAVES TO CEMETERIES IN VIRGINIA, GEORGIA, AND THE CAROLINAS.

Executive Mansion,

Washington,_____, 186_.

Four score and seven years ago our fathers brought forth, upon this continent, a new nation, conceived in liberty, and dedicated to the proposition that "all men are created equal"

Now we are engaged in a great civil war, testing whether that nation, or any nation so conceived, and so dedicated, can long endure. We are met on a great battle field of that war. We have come to dedicate a portion of it, as a final rest- ing place for those who died here, that the nation might live. This we may, in all propriety do. But, in a larger sense, we can not dedicate— we can not consecrate— we can not hallow, this ground— The brave men, living and dead, who struggled here, have hallowed it, far above our poor power to add or detract. The world will little note, nor long remember what we say here; while it can never forget what they did here.

It is rather for us, the living, to stand here, we here be dedica

ted to the great task remaining before us—
that, from these honored dead we take increased devotion to that cause for which
they here, gave the last full measure of devotion— that we here highly resolve these
dead shall not have died in vain; that
this nation, shall have a new birth of freedom, and that government of the people by
the people for. the people, shall not perish from the earth.

President Lincoln delivered the Gettysburg Address in this area, now a part of Evergreen Cemetery. The location is one hundred yards or less from the Soldiers' National Monument that can be seen in the background of the adjacent Soldiers' National Cemetery. The precise location of the speaker's platform from November 19, 1863, is unknown. The exact spot can be closely estimated, but not pinpointed with certainty.

The cast iron fence separating Evergreen Cemetery and the Soldiers' National Cemetery was standing in Lafayette Square in 1863, across from the Executive Mansion, when Abraham Lincoln was President. In 1888, legislation passed in Congress allowing the fence to be moved to Gettysburg. The fence was moved from Lafayette Square in Washington, D.C., to East Cemetery Hill in 1889 to decorate and enclose part of the hill.

IN 1933, THE LAFAYETTE SQUARE FENCE WAS MOVED FROM EAST CEMETERY HILL ACROSS THE BALTIMORE PIKE TO SEPARATE THE SOLDIERS' NATIONAL CEMETERY AND THE EVERGREEN CEMETERY, WHERE IT HAS REMAINED FOR EIGHTY YEARS. THE CROWD AT THE CEREMONY ON THE DAY OF DEDICATION, NOVEMBER 19, 1863, FILLED THIS ENTIRE AREA NEAR WHERE THE FENCE AND SOLDIERS' NATIONAL MONUMENT ARE CURRENTLY LOCATED.

LANDSCAPE ARCHITECT WILLIAM SAUNDERS DESIGNED THE CEMETERY AS A LARGE SEMI-CIRCLE,
RADIATING FROM A CENTRAL POINT WITH A GRAND MONUMENT (LATER THE SOLDIERS' NATIONAL MONUMENT).
THE CEMETERY'S SECTIONS ARE DIVIDED BY STATE. THE STATES WITH THE LARGEST NUMBER OF GRAVES ARE ON THE OUTER
PORTIONS OF THE SEMI-CIRCLE. REINTERMENTS FROM THE BATTLEFIELD TO THE CEMETERY CONTINUED THROUGH MARCH, 1864.

This urn memorial to the 1st Minnesota Regiment Volunteers in the cemetery
was the first completed stone monument on the entire Gettysburg battlefield.
Dedicated in 1867, the Soldiers' National Monument was dedicated soon after in 1869.
This is an impressive distinction, considering the Gettysburg battlefield is one of the most memorialized places
on earth. The marble monument to the 1st Minnesota has a line from the Gettysburg Address inscribed on its side.

OFFICERS AND ENLISTED MEN WERE BURIED SIDE BY SIDE, WITH NO SPECIAL DISTINCTION FOR RANK. PRESIDENT LINCOLN LIKED
THE DESIGN VERY MUCH BECAUSE ALL SOLDIERS ARE REPRESENTED EQUALLY. LANDSCAPE ARCHITECT WILLIAM SAUNDERS
CREATED A VERY PROGRESSIVE DESIGN FOR THE ERA. HE VERY EFFECTIVELY CONVEYS THE CONCEPT OF UNITY.

The Gettysburg Presbyterian Church has preserved the pew
where President Lincoln, Secretary of State Seward, and John Burns sat during the oration.
The Gettysburg Presbyterian Church is famous for another President. Dwight and Mamie Eisenhower were
members of the Presbyterian Church for over eight years when they lived next to the battlefield, near Gettysburg.

"is something out of my usual line, but a President of the United States has a multiplicity of duties not specified in the Constitution or acts of Congress. This is one of them. This money belongs to a poor Negro [Johnson] who is a porter in one of the departments [the Treasury] and who is at present very bad with the smallpox. He did not catch it from me, however; at least I think not. He is now in hospital and could not draw his pay because he could not sign his name. I have been at considerable trouble to overcome the difficulty and get it for him and have at length succeeded in cutting red tape . . . . I am now dividing the money and putting by a portion labeled, in an envelope, with my own hands, according to his wish."

That was not the only financial transaction that Lincoln performed for Johnson. With the President acting as his endorser, Johnson had obtained a $150 mortgage from the First National Bank of Washington to buy a house. Soon after Johnson's death, the bank's cashier, William J. Huntington, remarked to Lincoln: "the barber who used to shave you, I hear, is dead."

"Oh, yes," Lincoln said with some feeling, "William is gone. I bought a coffin for the poor fellow, and have had to help his family."

(Lincoln arranged to have Johnson buried in Arlington National Cemetery and paid for his funeral as well as his tombstone, which contains a simple inscription: "William H. Johnson, Citizen.")

When Huntington said the bank would forgive the loan, Lincoln replied emphatically: "No you don't. I endorsed the notes, and am bound to pay them; and it is your duty to make me pay them."

"Yes," said the banker, "but it has long been our custom to devote a portion of our profits to charitable objects; and this seems to be a most deserving one."

When the President demurred, Huntington said: "Well, Mr. Lincoln, I will tell you how we can arrange this. The loan to William was a joint one between you and the bank. You stand half of the loss, and I will cancel the other."

President Lincoln's special train departed the Gettysburg Train Station at around 7:00 P.M.

Previous to the address of the Hon. C. Anderson, Gov. Seymour presented a flag to a New York regiment, and made an appropriate speech.

We are also informed that just as the President was going to hear Mr. Anderson, a gentleman introduced to him old John Burns, the soldier of 1812, and the only man in Gettysburg who volunteered to defend it; and that the President invited him to go with him and Secretary Seward to hear the speech, and, each taking his arm, the old man between the two great statesmen for whom he had literally fought and bled, was escorted by them to the church, where he sat between them during the speaking. This little incident must have been a truly gratifying compliment to the brave old hero.

This we did not witness, as we were at the railroad endeavoring to get homewards. Nobody seemed to know anything of the arrangements, and thousands were patiently waiting to get home.

It appeared finally that the directors of the road or some other power had ordered that no train should leave until after the President's special train had gone, and hence, although the time for the regular train was 1 o'clock, and hundreds literally had thronged to the depot to go by that, yet they and additional expectants, until the accumulating hundreds had swelled to thousands, were all compelled to wait until near 7 o'clock, six mortal, long, wearying, slowly-dragging hours. We are confident that our excellent President was not a party to this shameful mismanagement, and that had he known that so dense a crowd of citizens were waiting upon his movements he would not have delayed another minute—but it was, nevertheless, the case, that while at least two full and heavy trains might have been run to Hanover Junction and back between 1 and half-past 5, P.M., yet one of the largest crowds that ever waited at a depot were detained here through a most unfortunate mistake. To the credit of our citizens be it said they bore their delay with remarkable patience, and the Baltimore Union Glee Club relieved the weariness of a very large portion by singing in a superior manner a constant succession of patriotic and popular songs.

It was my good fortune to return at last on the President's special train, conducted to Baltimore by Mr. John Vandanskee, who certainly deserved the thanks of many of the phonographic and funny graphic gentlemen on the train; for he courteously procured and fixed for them, at considerable trouble, an excellent light, around which, busy as bees, they compared notes and transcribed their phonographic reports for the papers for which they were laboring. Though neither a phono or funny grapher, he certainly obtained the thanks of your present correspondent.

The whole affair passed off admirably, saving the annoying and unnecessary railroad delays. There seemed an abundance to eat and drink; the crowd were of the best class of our American citizens, highly intelligent, refined, and of course quiet and orderly.

There seemed to me to be no sensible jar or discord to the whole proceedings. It struck me, however, that the flags upon the flagstaffs should have been at half-mast, and all should have been draped in black, especially those at Round Top and on the ground immediately in front of the platform. It appeared to me, too, that minute guns should have been fired from Round Top and Culp's Hill—at least from 9 until 4—throughout the day. Further than this there appeared nothing left undone that ought to have been done, and possibly there may exist ample reasons why the omissions I have indicated were permitted.

THE TRAIN ARRIVED AT WASHINGTON AT TEN MINUTES TO ONE ON FRIDAY MORNING, AND THUS ENDED
THE DEDICATION OF THE GETTYSBURG CEMETERY—A DAY LONG TO BE REMEMBERED BY THE GETTYSBURGHERS
IN THIS TO THEM EVENTFUL YEAR, AND ONE WHOSE EFFECTS WILL PASS INTO HISTORY.

JOHN HAY, PRESIDENT LINCOLN'S ASSISTANT PERSONAL SECRETARY AND PART-TIME CORRESPONDENT,
WASHINGTON <u>DAILY MORNING CHRONICLE</u>, NOVEMBER 21, 1863

PRESIDENT LINCOLN AND HIS ENTOURAGE ARRIVED BACK AT THE EXECUTIVE MANSION (THE WHITE HOUSE) AT 1:00 A.M.

ted to the great tas

that, from these hon

creased devotion to tha

they here, gave the l

votion — that we here

dead shall we her

remaining before us—

ed dead we take in-

cause for which

t full measure of ou-

highly resolve them

dead in vain; that

TRUTH AND MYTH SURROUNDING THE GETTYSBURG ADDRESS

IF I COULD FLATTER MYSELF—REACTIONS TO THE ADDRESS

As Everett noted, the President's handiwork was "greatly admired." Some commentators immediately recognized that Lincoln had produced a masterpiece, and Everett himself added his voice to the chorus of praise, writing with customary graciousness to Lincoln the day after the ceremony: "Permit me . . . to express my great admiration of the thoughts expressed by you, with such eloquent simplicity & appropriateness, at the consecration of the Cemetery. I should be glad, if I could flatter myself that I came as near to the central idea of the occasion, in two hours, as you did in two minutes." (Lincoln told his friend James Speed that "he had never received a compliment he prized more highly.")

Equally gracious, Lincoln replied: "In our respective parts yesterday, you could not have been excused to make a short address, nor I a long one. I am pleased to know that, in your judgment, the little I did say was not entirely a failure. Of course I knew Mr. Everett would not fail; and yet, while the whole discourse was eminently satisfactory, and will be of great value, there were passages in it which trancended my expectation. The point made against the theory of the general government being only an agency, whose principals are the States, was new to me, and, as I think, is one of the best arguments for the national supremacy. The tribute to our noble women for their angel-ministering to the suffering soldiers, surpasses, in its way, as do the subjects of it, whatever has gone before."

Though posterity has come to regard Lincoln's remarks as a terse, sublime masterpiece and Everett's oration as a florid, diffuse history lecture, the contemporary press devoted more coverage to the latter than to the former.

Democrats at the time, however, ridiculed Lincoln's speech. Some of them criticized the Gettysburg Address for injecting politics into a solemn, nonpartisan occasion. The leading Democratic journal of the Midwest, the Chicago Times, called it "an offensive exhibition of boorishness and vulgarity" and added that the "cheek of every American must tingle with shame as he reads the silly flat and dishwattery remarks of the man who has to be pointed out as the President of the United States." The Harrisburg Weekly Patriot and Union expressed similar contempt for the address and made a wildly inaccurate guess about its future: "We pass over the silly remarks of the President. For the credit of the nation we are willing that the veil of oblivion shall be dropped over them, and they shall be no more repeated or thought of."

Democrats criticized most vehemently the implication that the war was being fought, at least in part, to free the

My dear Sir: Nov. 20, 1863

Your kind note of to-day is received. In our respective parts yesterday, you could not have been excused to make a short address, nor I a long one. I am pleased to know that, in your judgment, the little I did say was not entirely a failure. Of course I knew Mr. Everett would not fail; and yet, while the whole discourse was eminently satisfactory, and will be of great value, there were passages in it which trancended my expectation. The point made against the theory of the general government being only an agency, whose principals are the States, was new to me, and, as I think, is one of the best arguments for the national supremacy. The tribute to our noble women for their angel-ministering to the suffering soldiers, surpasses, in its way, as do the subjects of it, whatever has gone before.

Our sick boy, for whom you kindly inquire, we hope is past the worst.
                                                    Your Obt. Servt.
                                                    A. Lincoln

LETTER TO EDWARD EVERETT, NOVEMBER 20, 1863

ON NOVEMBER 20, EDWARD EVERETT WROTE LINCOLN:

"NOT WISHING TO INTRUDE UPON YOUR PRIVACY, WHEN YOU MUST BE MUCH ENGAGED, I BEG LEAVE, IN THIS WAY, TO THANK YOU VERY SINCERELY FOR YOUR GREAT THOUGHTFULNESS FOR MY DAUGHTER'S ACCOMMODATION ON THE PLATFORM YESTERDAY, & MUCH KINDNESS OTHERWISE TO ME & MINE AT GETTYSBURG."

"PERMIT ME ALSO TO EXPRESS MY GREAT ADMIRATION OF THE THOUGHTS EXPRESSED BY YOU, WITH SUCH ELOQUENT SIMPLICITY & APPROPRIATENESS, AT THE CONSECRATION OF THE CEMETERY. I SHOULD BE GLAD, IF I COULD FLATTER MYSELF THAT I CAME AS NEAR TO THE CENTRAL IDEA OF THE OCCASION, IN TWO HOURS, AS YOU DID IN TWO MINUTES. MY SON WHO PARTED FROM ME AT BALTIMORE & MY DAUGHTER, CONCUR IN THIS SENTIMENT. . . ."

"I HOPE YOUR ANXIETY FOR YOUR CHILD WAS RELIEVED ON YOUR ARRIVAL."

"TAD" LINCOLN HAD BEEN SICK WHEN LINCOLN WENT TO GETTYSBURG ON NOVEMBER 18, AND LINCOLN WAS ILL WITH VARIOLOID FOR SEVERAL DAYS FOLLOWING HIS RETURN TO WASHINGTON, D.C.

slaves. (Though Lincoln did not say so explicitly, that was the evident meaning of his references to a "new birth of freedom" and to equality.) "We submit that Lincoln did most foully traduce the motives of the men who were slain at Gettysburg," protested the Chicago <u>Times</u>. "They gave their lives to maintain the old government, and the old constitution and Union." After citing passages in the Constitution alluding to slavery, the editor argued that "Mr. Lincoln occupies his present position by virtue of this Constitution, and is sworn to the maintenance and enforcement of these provisions. It was to uphold this constitution, and the Union created by it, that our officers and soldiers gave their lives at Gettysburg. How dare he, then, standing on their graves, misstate the cause for which they died, and libel the statesmen who founded the government? They were men possessing too much self-respect to declare negroes were their equals, or were entitled to equal privileges." The New York <u>World</u> maintained that "the Constitution not merely does not say one word about equal rights, but expressly admits the idea of inequality of human rights." In Keene, New Hampshire, the <u>Cheshire Republican</u> indignantly declared: "If it was to establish negro equality that our soldiers lost their lives, Mr. Lincoln should have said so before. These soldiers won the day at Gettysburg under the noble impulse that they were contending for the Constitution and the Union."

Democrats also objected to what they considered poor taste in Lincoln's opening sentence. It was "questionable," said the New York <u>World</u>, to represent "the 'fathers' in the stages of conception and parturition." Similarly, the Boston <u>Daily Courier</u> protested against the "obstetric allusion."

British opinion was not uniformly favorable. The London <u>Times</u> correspondent said "[a]nything more dull and commonplace it wouldn't be easy to produce."

LARGE BOULDERS NEXT TO A STONE WALL AT "THE ANGLE" RUN ALONG CEMETERY RIDGE, AS THE GROUND SLOPES TO SEMINARY RIDGE TO THE WEST. THIS VIEW STRAIGHT SOUTH INCLUDES BIG ROUND TOP ON THE LEFT AND THE CATOCTIN MOUNTAINS IN THE FAR DISTANCE. THE CONFEDERATES BROKE THE UNION LINES SEVERAL TIMES DURING THREE DAYS OF BATTLE—THE LAST TIME AT THIS LOCATION. AFTER THE FEDERAL TROOPS DROVE THEM BACK, THE GREAT BATTLE WAS OVER.

SOBS OF SMOTHERED EMOTION—
APPRECIATION FOR THE ADDRESS BY LINCOLN'S CONTEMPORARIES

Some consider John Hay's rather perfunctory diary entry ("the President in a firm free way, with more grace than is his wont said his half dozen words lines of consecration") emblematic of a supposedly lukewarm public reaction to the Gettysburg Address. (Gabor Boritt stresses this point in his book, The Gettysburg Gospel). But in fact, as Hay's report in the Washington Daily Morning Chronicle indicates, many listeners and readers did appreciate that Lincoln had crafted an exceptional speech. In his November 19 dispatch to the Washington Daily Morning Chronicle, Hay noted that the President's "address, though short, glittered with gems, evincing the gentleness and goodness of heart peculiar to him."

The first two paragraphs on page 144 include Edward Everett's compelling letter he sent to Lincoln the day after the ceremony. This is an extraordinary response from the main speaker of the event who had received much of the attention from the day and who was considered the great orator of the era.

In addition to Everett and Hay, others in the audience were profoundly moved. Isaac Jackson Allen of the Columbus Ohio State Journal reported that Lincoln's "calm but earnest utterance of this deep and beautiful address stirred the deepest fountains of feeling and emotion in the hearts of the vast throngs before him; and when he had concluded, scarcely could an untearful eye be seen, while sobs of smothered emotion were heard on every hand." When the President said that the "world will little note nor long remember what we say here, but it can never forget what they did here," a captain who had lost an arm "burst all restraint; and burying his face in his handkerchief, he sobbed aloud while his manly frame shook with no unmanly emotion. In a few moments, with a stern struggle to master his emotions, he lifted his still streaming eyes to heaven and in a low and solemn tone exclaimed, 'God Almighty bless Abraham Lincoln!'" Allen termed Lincoln's speech "the best word of his administration," and accurately predicted that it "will live long after many more elaborate and pretentious utterances shall have been forgotten."

Other journalists and editors recognized that Lincoln had produced a masterpiece. The Philadelphia Press correspondent called it a "brief, but immortal speech," and that paper ran an editorial describing the occasion as "sublime; certainly the ruler of the nation never stood higher, and grander, and more prophetic." Another Philadelphia journal, the Evening Bulletin, remarked that the "President's brief speech is most happily expressed. It is warm, earnest, unaffected and touching." The Chicago Tribune reporter declared that the "dedicatory remarks of President Lincoln will live among the annals of man." Elsewhere in the Midwest, the Cincinnati Gazette deemed it "the right thing, in the right place, and a perfect thing in every respect."

Reverend Sir, and Ladies and Gentlemen: I accept, with emotions of profoundest gratitude, the beautiful gift you have been pleased to present to me. You will, of course, expect that I acknowledge it. So much has been said about Gettysburg, and so well said, that for me to attempt to say more may, perhaps, only serve to weaken the force of that which has already been said. A most graceful and eloquent tribute was paid to the patriotism and selfdenying labors of the American ladies, on the occasion of the consecration of the National Cemetery at Gettysburg, by our illustrious friend, Edward Everett, now, alas! departed from earth. His life was a truly great one, and, I think, the greatest part of it was that which crowned its closing years. I wish you to read, if you have not already done so, the glowing, and eloquent, and truthful words which he then spoke of the women of America. Truly, the services they have rendered to the defenders of our country in this perilous time, and are yet rendering, can never be estimated as they ought to be.

For your kind wishes to me, personally, I beg leave to render you, likewise, my sincerest thanks. I assure you they are reciprocated. And now, gentlemen and ladies, may God bless you all.

EXTEMPORANEOUS SPEECH (REPLY TO PHILADELPHIA DELEGATION)
JANUARY 24, 1865

WASHINGTON DAILY MORNING CHRONICLE, JANUARY 25, 1865. LINCOLN REPLIED TO A SPEECH OF REVEREND WILLIAM SUDDARDS, DELIVERED ON PRESENTING "A TRULY BEAUTIFUL AND SUPERB VASE OF SKELETON LEAVES, GATHERED FROM THE BATTLE-FIELDS OF GETTYSBURG." EDWARD EVERETT DIED ON JANUARY 15, 1865.

Men of letters were equally enthusiastic. Josiah G. Holland of the Springfield, Massachusetts, Republican wrote that "the rhetorical honors of the occasion were won by President Lincoln. His little speech is a perfect gem; deep in feeling, compact in thought and expression, and tasteful and elegant in every word and comma. Then it has the merit of unexpectedness in its verbal perfection and beauty. We had grown so accustomed to homely and imperfect phrase in his productions that we had come to think it was the law of his utterance. But this shows he can talk handsomely as well as act sensibly. Turn back and read it over, it will repay study as a model speech. Strong feelings and a large brain were its parents."

The speech won over some others who had been critical of Lincoln's rhetoric. In August 1863, Charles King Newcomb, a Transcendentalist poet whom Ralph Waldo Emerson admired, bemoaned the President's "want of eloquence." But on November 23, after reading the Gettysburg Address, Newcomb concluded that "Lincoln is, doubtless, the greatest orator of the age: a point not generally seen."

The editor of the Providence Journal, James Burrill Angell, former chairman of the Modern Languages Department at Brown University and future president of the University of Vermont (and later the University of Michigan), confessed that he did not know "where to look for a more admirable speech than the brief one which the President made at the close of Mr. Everett's oration. It is often said that the hardest thing in the world is to make a five minute speech. But could the most elaborate and splendid oration be more beautiful, more touching, more inspiring than those few words of the President? They had in my humble judgement the charm and power of the very highest eloquence."

George William Curtis, editor of Harpers Weekly, thought that the "few words of the President went from the heart to the heart. They cannot be read, even, without kindling emotion. . . . It was as simple and felicitous and earnest a word as was ever spoken." More extravagantly, he called the Gettysburg Address the "most perfect piece of American eloquence, and as noble and pathetic and appropriate as the oration of Pericles over the Peloponnesian dead."

THE CONFEDERATES BREACHED THE UNION LINE ALONG CEMETERY RIDGE AT "THE ANGLE" ON THE LAST DAY OF THE BATTLE.
THIS POINT AT WHICH THE UNION SOLDIERS STOPPED LEE'S ASSAULT WAS REFERRED TO AS THE "HIGH-WATER MARK OF THE
CONFEDERACY" BY A WELL-KNOWN BATTLEFIELD HISTORIAN JOHN BADGER BACHELDER, NOT LONG AFTER THE BATTLE.
BACHELDER PRODUCED A WELL-KNOWN MAP OF THE BATTLEFIELD IN 1863 WHICH IS INCLUDED ON PAGES 193 AND 194.

A Pithy Reminder—the Crowd's Reaction

Ward Hill Lamon, a close friend of Lincoln who served as chief marshal and master of ceremonies at Gettysburg, quoted the President's words uttered just after he delivered the address: "Lamon, that speech won't scour!" Lamon explained that the "word 'scour' he often used in expressing his positive conviction that a thing lacked merit." But an examination of Lincoln's writings reveals that he did <u>not</u> use "scour" to indicate "that a thing lacked merit." Lamon, however, did so; in his reminiscences, he reported that he criticized the President's decision to grow a beard, telling him: "It won't scour." When Lamon grew a mustache, Lincoln returned the favor, remarking: "That won't work." Lamon replied, "Shoot that beard, Lincoln – it won't scour." So it is highly likely that Lamon was putting words in the mouth of the President, who did not in fact say that his speech "won't scour."

But even if he did not use the word "scour," did Lincoln have reason to think his audience was unimpressed? Lamon reported that Lincoln followed his "scour" remark with this sentence: "It is a flat failure and the people are disappointed." Did in fact the huge crowd fail to applaud? The Associated Press noted that the audience applauded the speech at five different points and at its conclusion gave "long-continued applause." The New York <u>Times</u> reported that when Lincoln finished speaking, "Three cheers were then given for the President and the Governors of the States." A member of the audience, however, wrote shortly after the event that when Lincoln "finished speaking the people were silent for a time[,] many not knowing his speech was finished."

So it is possible that Lincoln did in fact think his remarks had failed to impress the crowd, but he may not have minded, for he knew it would be widely published and thus serve as a pithy reminder to his constituents of the war's central purpose and thus encourage them to persevere in that noble struggle.

PRESIDENT LINCOLN PASSED BY
THIS TREE ON NOVEMBER 19, 1863
C.W.R.T. 1978

This plaque is in front of the giant sycamore tree in Alumni Park on Baltimore Street.
A new plaque has been placed in front of the other 180-year-old witness tree—
the remaining twin sycamore directly in front of the Winebrenner house.

In 1920, the iconoclastic journalist and essayist H. L. Mencken praised the form of the Gettysburg Address but criticized its substance: "The Gettysburg speech was at once the shortest and the most famous oration in American history." It contains "the highest emotion reduced to a few poetical phrases. Lincoln himself never even remotely approached it. It is genuinely stupendous. But let us not forget that it is poetry, not logic; beauty, not sense. Think of the argument in it. Put it into the cold words of everyday. The doctrine is simply this: that the Union soldiers who died at Gettysburg sacrificed their lives to the cause of self-determination – that government of the people, by the people, for the people, should not perish from the earth. It is difficult to imagine anything more untrue. The Union soldiers in the battle actually fought against self-determination; it was the Confederates who fought for the right of their people to govern themselves."

In 1854, Lincoln addressed this question in his first major anti-slavery speech. Before a large audience in Peoria, Illinois, he denounced Stephen A. Douglas's "popular sovereignty" version of self-determination. Douglas claimed that if Congress or the courts forbade settlers who moved into America's western territories to bring slaves with them, the principle of self-government would be violated. Lincoln responded: "The doctrine of self government is right – absolutely and eternally right – but it has no just application, as here attempted. Or perhaps I should rather say that whether it has such just application depends upon whether a negro is <u>not</u> or <u>is</u> a man. If he is <u>not</u> a man, why in that case, he who <u>is</u> a man may, as a matter of self-government, do just as he pleases with him. But if the negro <u>is</u> a man, is it not to that extent, a total destruction of self-government, to say that he too shall not govern <u>himself</u>? When the white man governs himself that is self-government; but when he governs himself, and also governs <u>another</u> man, that is <u>more</u> than self-government – that is despotism. If the negro is a <u>man</u>, why then my ancient faith teaches me that 'all men are created equal;' and that there can be no moral right in connection with one man's making a slave of another. . . . no man is good enough to govern another man, <u>without that other's consent</u>. I say this is the leading principle – the sheet anchor of American republicanism." He added: "Nearly eighty years ago we began by declaring that all men are created equal; but now from that beginning we have run down to the other declaration, that for some men to enslave others is 'a sacred right of self-government.'"

Throughout his 1858 debates with Senator Douglas, Lincoln insisted that the Declaration of Independence's assertion that "all men are created equal" covered blacks as well as whites. Douglas, who incessantly appealed to the deep-seated race prejudice of the Illinois electorate, denied that claim: "I hold that the signers of the Declaration of Independence had no reference to negroes at all when they declared all men to be created equal. They did not mean negro, nor the savage Indians, nor the Fejee Islanders, nor any other barbarous race. They were speaking of white men. They alluded to men of European birth and European descent – to white men, and to none others, when they declared that doctrine. I hold that this government was established on the white basis. It was established by white men for the benefit of white men and their posterity forever, and should be administered by white men, and none others."

In 1858, responding to a speech by Douglas, Lincoln boldly declared: "Let us discard all this quibbling about this man and the other man – this race and that race and the other race being inferior, and therefore they must be placed in an inferior position – discarding our standard that they [the founding fathers] have left us. Let us discard all these things, and unite as one people throughout this land, until we shall once more stand up declaring that all men are created equal."

The doctrine of self government is right—absolutely and eternally right—but it has no just application, as here attempted. Or perhaps I should rather say that whether it has such just application depends upon whether a negro is not or is a man. If he is not a man, why in that case, he who is a man may, as a matter of self-government, do just as he pleases with him. But if the negro is a man, is it not to that extent, a total destruction of self-government, to say that he too shall not govern himself? When the white man governs himself that is self-government; but when he governs himself, and also governs another man, that is more than self-government—that is despotism. If the negro is a man, why then my ancient faith teaches me that "all men are created equal;" and that there can be no moral right in connection with one man's making a slave of another. . . .

. . . Near eighty years ago we began by declaring that all men are created equal; but now from that beginning we have run down to the other declaration, that for some men to enslave others is a "sacred right of self-government." These principles can not stand together. They are as opposite as God and mammon; and whoever holds to the one, must despise the other.

SPEECH IN PEORIA, ILLINOIS, OCTOBER 16, 1854

a new birth of freedom—A New Direction of Ideals
November 19, 1863

Garry Wills maintained that in the Gettysburg Address, "Slavery was not mentioned, because he [Lincoln] wanted to lift his ideal of America as the Declaration's nation above divisive particulars." Gary W. Gallagher observed that when Lincoln "spoke of 'a new birth of freedom,' many listeners (and later readers) would have conjured images not of ending slavery but of guaranteeing and extending their own liberty and freedom, through political action and economic promise, to shape and benefit from a Union where the cards were not stacked against common people." Similarly, Gabor Boritt wrote: "Lincoln needed the masses in the middle. Equating his use of Jefferson's words with the rights of black people was only one possible interpretation. Many did not understand the President's words in those terms. Equality could carry civil, economic, social, or racial connotations. To middle-of-the-road folk, the liberty he spoke about could be the white man's liberty."

Yet many of Lincoln's contemporaries, especially Democrats, <u>did</u> interpret his remarks about "a new birth of freedom" as a reference to emancipation. Samuel Medary of the Columbus, Ohio, <u>Crisis</u> sneeringly wrote that "the President read a mawkish harrangue about this 'war for freedom' of the negro by the destruction of the liberties of American citizens." The leading Democratic journal in the Midwest, the Chicago <u>Times</u>, charged that "Lincoln did most foully traduce the motives of the men who were slain at Gettysburg. They gave their lives to maintain the old government, and the old Constitution and Union." After citing passages in the Constitution alluding to slavery, the editor argued that "Mr. Lincoln occupies his present position by virtue of this Constitution, and is sworn to the maintenance and enforcement of these provisions. It was to uphold this Constitution, and the Union created by it, that our officers and soldiers gave their lives at Gettysburg. How dare he, then, standing on their graves, misstate the cause for which they died, and libel the statesmen who founded the government? They were men possessing too much self-respect to declare negroes were their equals, or were entitled to equal privileges." A leading eastern Democratic paper, the New York <u>World</u>, maintained that "the Constitution not merely does not say one word about equal rights, but expressly admits the idea of inequality of human rights."

In all likelihood, Lincoln intended his reference to "a new birth of freedom" to be understood as an allusion to emancipation, and the words immediately following ("government of the people, by the people, and for the people") as a vindication of popular government. Like Daniel Webster, he viewed the preservation of the union and the promotion of freedom as complementary, not mutually exclusive.

As noted above, on the night before the dedication ceremony, Seward spoke briefly to a crowd, stressing both the importance of emancipation and the preservation of free government. It seems likely that the secretary of state had prepared his remarks to be delivered at the cemetery in case Lincoln had to cancel his appearance. It also seems likely that Seward would have consulted with the President about his text. If Lincoln had not wanted slavery mentioned, Seward would probably not have spoken so emphatically about it.

THE MOON SETS IN THE WEST AS THE EARLY SUN RISES OVER CEMETERY RIDGE—
FROM THE LYDIA LEISTER FARM, GENERAL MEADE'S HEADQUARTERS DURING THE BATTLE.

A Giant (If Benign) Swindle—Cleansing the Constitution

Garry Wills, author of the Pulitzer Prize-winning book <u>Lincoln at Gettysburg</u>, argues that Lincoln "stealthily . . . remade America" by surreptitiously bootlegging the concept of equality into the Constitution, which does not contain that word. According to Wills, the President went to Gettysburg "to clear the infected atmosphere of American history itself, tainted with official sins and inherited guilt." He sought to "cleanse the Constitution" by altering that document "from within, by appeal from its letter to the spirit, subtly changing the recalcitrant stuff of that legal compromise." By doing this implicitly, "he performed one of the most daring acts of open-air sleight of hand ever witnessed by the unsuspecting." Each member of his audience "was having his or her intellectual pocket picked." The assembled multitude "departed with a new thing in its ideological luggage, the new Constitution Lincoln had substituted for the one they had brought there with them."

Wills quotes the Chicago <u>Times</u> of November 23, 1863, (previously noted on page 156), which, after citing the three provisions of the Constitution alluding to slavery, argued against Lincoln in favor of racist views. Wills says the Chicago editors astutely "recognized the audacity of Lincoln's undertaking." So too, Wills claims, did the conservative commentator Willmoore Kendall, who charged that Lincoln "attempted a new act of founding, involving concretely a startling new interpretation of that principle of the founders which declared that 'all men are created equal'." Wills writes that Kendall, the Chicago <u>Times</u>, and other critics of Lincoln correctly viewed the Gettysburg Address as a "giant (if benign) swindle."

But was it? Did Lincoln really slip equality into the Constitution, unbeknownst to his contemporaries? No, he did not. Equality became part of the Constitution five years after the Gettysburg Address with the ratification of the Fourteenth Amendment, which provided (among other things) that "No state shall . . . deny to any person within its jurisdiction the equal protection of the laws." The adoption of the amendment was not a result of Lincoln's speech at Gettysburg; it was passed and ratified because white Southerners after the Civil War had, in effect, attempted to re-enslave blacks by instituting for them a separate set of laws known as "black codes." In 1866, the Republican-dominated Congress passed a Civil Rights Act designed to overturn such codes, and the Fourteenth Amendment was adopted in 1868 to make sure that when the Democrats regained power, they could not easily reinstitute black codes, for instead of merely repealing a statute, they would have to amend the Constitution.

A QUIET, EARLY JULY SUNRISE ON CEMETERY RIDGE.

Set Apart These Grounds To Their Sacred Use—Lincoln's Invitation

On November 2, the chief organizer of the ceremony, David Wills, extended this invitation to Lincoln:

"The Several States having Soldiers in the Army of the Potomac, who were killed at the Battle of Gettysburg, or have since died at the various hospitals which were established in the vicinity, have procured grounds on a prominent part of the Battle Field for a Cemetery, and are having the dead removed to them and properly buried."

"These Grounds will be Consecrated and set apart to this Sacred purpose, by appropriate Ceremonies, on Thursday, the 19th instant. Hon Edward Everett will deliver the Oration. I am authorized by the Governors of the different States to invite you to be present, and participate in these Ceremonies, which will doubtless be very imposing and solemnly impressive."

"It is the desire that, after the Oration, you, as Chief Executive of the Nation, formally set apart these grounds to their Sacred use by a few appropriate remarks. It will be a source of great gratification to the many widows and orphans that have been made almost friendless by the Great Battle here, to have you here personally; and it will kindle anew in the breasts of the Comrades of these brave dead, who are now in the tented field or nobly meeting the foe in the front, a confidence that they who sleep in death on the Battle Field are not forgotten by those highest in Authority; and they will feel that, should their fate be the same, their remains will not be uncared for."

"We hope you will be able to be present to perform this last solemn act to the Soldiers dead on this Battle Field."

"I am with great Respect, Your Excellency's Obedient Servant, David Wills, Agent for A. G. Curtin Gov. of Penna. and acting for all the States."

Because Edward Everett's invitation was sent on September 23, some have inferred that Wills rather presumptuously asked Lincoln to participate as an afterthought. But the President probably knew weeks earlier that he would receive such an invitation, for on October 11 Wills told a journalist that "President Lincoln is expected to perform the consecrational service." Lincoln may well have been approached even earlier, perhaps by Pennsylvania Governor Andrew G. Curtin, who spoke with the President on August 28. Curtin led the movement to establish the cemetery.

An early July sunrise on Cemetery Ridge the next morning as storm clouds approach.

Lincoln drafted the Gettysburg Address in Washington and revised it in Gettysburg, but on the train conveying him from the capital to Pennsylvania he did not work on it. His principal White House secretary, John G. Nicolay, who accompanied Lincoln on the train ride, insisted that there "is neither record, evidence, nor well-founded tradition that Mr. Lincoln did any writing, or made any notes, on the journey between Washington and Gettysburg." On that four-car train "either composition or writing would have been extremely troublesome amid all the movement, the noise, the conversation, the greetings, and the questionings which ordinary courtesy required him to undergo in these surroundings." Moreover, "the rockings and joltings of the train" would have made "writing virtually impossible."

The best account we have of the composition of the address is one Lincoln himself gave to his good friend James Speed, who would become U.S. attorney general in 1864. Fifteen years later, Speed recounted a conversation he had with the President several months after the ceremony at Gettysburg: "The day before he left Washington he found time to write about half the speech. He took what he had written with him to Gettysburg, then he was put in the upper room of a house, and he asked to be left alone for a time. He then prepared the speech, but concluded it so shortly before it was to be delivered [that] he had not time to memorize it."

In 1878, another friend of Lincoln, the journalist Noah Brooks (who was slated to serve as Lincoln's personal secretary during the President's second term), recollected that in early November 1863 he accompanied the President on a visit to the photographic studio of Alexander Gardner: "Just as we were going down the stairs of the White House, the President suddenly remembered that he needed a paper, and, after hurrying back to his office, soon rejoined me with a long envelop in his hand. When we were fairly started, he said that in the envelope was an advance copy of Edward Everett's address to be delivered at the Gettysburg dedication on the following Tuesday. Drawing it out, I saw that it was a one-page supplement to a Boston paper, and that Mr. Everett's address nearly covered both sides of the sheet. The President expressed his admiration for the thoughtfulness of the Boston orator, who had sent this copy of his address in order that Mr. Lincoln might not traverse the same lines that the chosen speaker of the great occasion might have laid out for himself. When I exclaimed at its length, the President laughed and quoted the line: 'Solid men of Boston, make no long orations,' which he said he had met somewhere in a speech by Daniel Webster. He said that there was no danger that he should get upon the lines of Mr. Everett's oration, for what he had ready to say was very short, or, as he emphatically expressed it, 'short, short, short.' In reply to a question as to the speech having been already written, he said that it was written, 'but not finished.'" (A decade later, Brooks quoted Lincoln somewhat differently: "My speech is all blocked out. It is very short." And in 1895, he recalled Lincoln saying that the speech was written "but not finished.")

Some scholars have dismissed Brooks's accounts, for they contain some improbable assertions, but those accounts do plausibly tend to confirm Speed's statement that Lincoln had begun drafting the speech in Washington and that it was not completed by the time he departed for Gettysburg.

Another friend of Lincoln, Ward Hill Lamon, recalled that shortly before the President departed for Gettysburg, he "told me he would be expected to make a speech on the occasion – that he was extremely busy and had no time to prepare himself for it and feared he would be unable to do himself and the subject justice." The President then read aloud a draft of his speech, which Lamon thought was more or less the text of the speech Lincoln delivered on November 19. (The Indiana politico and public printer of the United States, John D. Defrees, also remembered that before Lincoln left Washington, he read Defrees "the famous Gettysburg speech.")

John G. Nicolay recalled that as the President boarded the train on November 18, he "carried in his pocket the autograph manuscript of so much of his address as he had written at Washington the day before." (In fact, it seems probable that he began writing it on November 15 or 16.)

On the evening of November 18, after the President had settled in at the Gettysburg home of David Wills, he evidently worked on the speech for a while, then called on Secretary of State William Henry Seward, who was lodging at a nearby house. Lincoln probably asked Seward's advice about the speech, just as he had done with his first inaugural address.

The next day, he continued tinkering with the document. Nicolay recalled going that morning "to the upper room in the house of Mr. Wills which Mr. Lincoln occupied, to report for duty, and remained with the President while he finished writing the Gettysburg Address."

Lincoln had long regarded the war as a struggle to vindicate "government of the people, by the people, and for the people." When less than a month after the outbreak of hostilities John Hay told him that many correspondents wished him to abolish slavery, he replied: "For my own part, I consider the central idea pervading this struggle is the necessity that is upon us, of proving that popular government is not an absurdity. We must settle this question now, whether in a free government the minority have the right to break up the government whenever they choose. If we fail it will go far to prove the incapability of the people to govern themselves." Alluding to slavery, he added: "There may be one consideration used in stay of such final judgment, but that is not for us to use in advance. That is, that there exists in our case, an instance of a vast and far reaching disturbing element, which the history of no other free nation will probably ever present. That however is not for us to say at present. Taking the government as we found it we will see if the majority can preserve it."

That same day, Lincoln addressed a letter to the Regent Captains of the tiny principality of San Marino, Italy, in which he said that the war "involves the question whether a Representative republic, extended and aggrandized so much as to be safe against foreign enemies can save itself from the dangers of domestic faction."

In his emphasis on the importance of preserving the Union and thereby vindicating both democracy and the rule of law, Lincoln accurately reflected the sentiment of most Northern supporters of the war. Like Daniel Webster, they fervently believed that "Liberty and Union" were "now and forever, one and inseparable."

Lincoln elaborated on this theme in his message to Congress of July 4, 1861. "Our popular government," he wrote, "has often been called an experiment. Two points in it our people have already settled – the successful establishing and the successful administering of it. One still remains – it's successful maintenance against a formidable attempt to overthrow it. It is now for them to demonstrate to the world, that those who can fairly carry an election, can also suppress a rebellion; that ballots are the rightful, and peaceful, successors of bullets; and that when ballots have fairly, and constitutionally decided, there can be no successful appeal back to bullets; that there can be no successful appeal, except to ballots themselves, at succeeding elections. Such will be a great lesson of peace; teaching men that what they cannot take by an election, neither can they take it by a war; teaching all, the folly of being the beginners of a war."

Later in the message, Lincoln foreshadowed the Gettysburg Address: "And this issue embraces more than the fate of these United States. It presents to the whole family of man the question, whether a Constitutional republic, or a democracy – a government of the people, by the same people – can, or cannot, maintain its territorial integrity against its own domestic foes. It presents the question, whether discontented individuals, too few in numbers to control administration, according to organic law, in any case, can always, upon the pretences made in this case, or on any other pretences, or arbitrarily, without any pretence, break up their government, and thus practically put an end to free government upon the earth. It forces us to ask: 'Is there, in all republics, this inherent and fatal weakness?' 'Must a government, of necessity, be too strong for the liberties of its own people, or too weak to maintain its own existence?'"

In the most eloquent passage of the message to Congress, Lincoln called the war "essentially a People's contest." For Unionists, "it is a struggle for maintaining in the world, that form and substance of government, whose leading object is, to elevate the condition of men – to lift artificial weights from all shoulders; to clear the paths of laudable pursuit for all; to afford all, an unfettered start, and a fair chance, in the race of life. Yielding to partial and temporary departures, from necessity, this is the leading object of the government for whose existence we contend."

On July 7, 1863, Lincoln gave a speech directly foreshadowing the address he would give four months later at Gettysburg: "How long ago is it? – eighty odd years – since on the Fourth of July for the first time in the history of the world a nation by its representatives, assembled and declared as a self-evident truth that 'all men are created equal.' That was the birthday of the United States of America. Since then the Fourth of July has had several peculiar recognitions. The two most distinguished men in the framing and support of the Declaration were Thomas Jefferson and John Adams – the one having penned it and the other sustained it the most forcibly in debate – the only two of the fifty-five who sustained [signed?] it being elected President of the United States. Precisely fifty years after they put their hands to the paper it pleased Almighty God to take both from the stage of action. This was indeed an extraordinary and remarkable event in our history. Another President, five years after, was called from this stage of existence on the same day and month of the year; and now, on this last Fourth of July just passed, when we have a gigantic Rebellion, at the bottom of which is an effort to overthrow the principle that all men were created equal, we have the surrender of a most powerful position and army on that very day [the city of Vicksburg, Mississippi, and the Confederate Army commanded by General John Pemberton], and not only so, but in a succession of battles in [Gettysburg,] Pennsylvania, near to us, through three days, so rapidly fought that they might be called one great battle on the 1st, 2d and 3d of the month of July; and on the 4th the cohorts of those who opposed the declaration that all men are created equal, 'turned tail' and run. Gentlemen, this is a glorious theme, and the occasion for a speech, but I am not prepared to make one worthy of the occasion."

So for at least several months Lincoln had been thinking about "a speech worthy of the occasion" when Union armies defeated those forces trying to "overthrow the principle that all men were created equal." He told James Speed that "he was eager to go" to Gettysburg "and desired to be prepared to say some appropriate thing."

(In August 1864, Lincoln repeated the gist of the Gettysburg Address when he told a regiment of Union troops: "I almost always feel inclined, when I happen to say anything to soldiers, to impress upon them in a few brief remarks the importance of success in this contest. It is not merely for to-day, but for all time to come that we should perpetuate for our children's children this great and free government, which we have enjoyed all our lives. I beg you to remember this, not merely for my sake, but for yours. I happen temporarily to occupy this big White House. I am a living witness that any one of your children may look to come here as my father's child has. It is in order that each of you may have through this free government which we have enjoyed, an open field and a fair chance for your industry, enterprise and intelligence; that you may have equal privileges in the race of life, with all its desirable human aspirations. It is for this the struggle should be maintained, that we may not lose our birthright — not only for one, but for two or three years. The nation is worth fighting for, to secure such an inestimable jewel.")

The progression of a beautiful, tranquil evening in July at the Soldiers' National Cemetery.
Governor Andrew Curtin's agent, attorney David Wills, acquired the land for the Commonwealth of Pennsylvania,
commissioned the landscape architect, William Saunders, and contracted for the reinterments. The cemetery was
officially named the Soldiers' National Cemetery—a national cemetery owned by the state of Pennsylvania.

Originating in 1863 as a state-owned "national cemetery", it was later transferred to the federal government. Following the Civil War, the U.S. Government began a process to establish a national cemetery system. Pennsylvania ceded the cemetery to the War Department in 1872. In 1933, the responsibility of the cemetery was transferred from the Department of War to the National Park Service in the Department of the Interior.

Congress officially established the national cemetery system, and the Soldiers' National Cemetery additionally became known as Gettysburg National Cemetery. After the Civil War, 303,536 Union soldiers were reinterred in 74 new national cemeteries. The process of developing cemeteries for Confederate soldiers in the South had a slow beginning after the war. As of 2013, there are 147 national cemeteries in the United States and Puerto Rico.

The National Park Service maintains 14 national cemeteries located within larger park units, including Gettysburg. The Department of Veterans Affairs' National Cemetery Administration maintains 131 national cemeteries in 39 states and Puerto Rico. The Department of the Army maintains two national cemeteries, the Arlington National Cemetery and the U.S. Soldiers' & Airmen's Home National Cemetery.

THREESCORE YEARS AND TEN—LITERARY SOURCES INSPIRING LINCOLN

When composing his speech, Lincoln doubtless recalled the language of Daniel Webster. One day during the Civil War, John Hay heard Lincoln and Secretary of State William Henry Seward discussing Webster. Hay recorded the conversation in his diary: "Seward said he [Webster] would not live, nor [Henry] Clay, a tithe as long as J[ohn] Q[uincy] Adams. The President disagreed with him, and thought Webster will be read forever." In Webster's celebrated 1830 second reply to Robert Y. Hayne, which Lincoln considered "the very best speech ever delivered," the Massachusetts senator referred to the "people's government, made for the people, made by the people, and answerable to the people."

In Lincoln's House Divided speech, delivered at Springfield in 1858, he evidently had Webster's reply to Hayne in mind. Lincoln began by saying: "If we could first know where we are, and whither we are tending, we could then better judge what to do, and how to do it." That sentence resembles Webster's opening lines: "When the mariner has been tossed for many days in thick weather, and on an unknown sea, he naturally avails himself of the first pause in the storm, the earliest glance of the sun, to take his latitude, and ascertain how far the elements have driven him from his true course. Let us imitate this prudence, and, before we float farther on the waves of this debate, refer to the point from which we departed, that we may at least be able to conjecture where we now are."

Later in his House Divided speech, Lincoln echoed Webster's reply to Hayne, describing his Republican party colleagues as a combination of "strange, discordant, and even, hostile elements," facing an enemy "wavering, dissevered and belligerent." This passage calls to mind Webster's allusion to "States dissevered, discordant, belligerent."

In all probability, as Lincoln composed the Gettysburg Address, he also thought of the words spoken by the eminent Unitarian divine, Theodore Parker, whom the President admired and who frequently corresponded with Lincoln's law partner, William H. Herndon. Parker used a definition of democracy similar to Webster's, and Lincoln was familiar with at least two of Parker's formulations. In his "Sermon on the Dangers which Threaten the Rights of Man in America," delivered on July 2, 1854, the minister twice referred to "government of all, by all, and for all." In another sermon delivered four years later, "The Effect of Slavery on the American People," Parker said: "Democracy is Direct Self-government, over all the people, for all the people, by all the people." Lincoln, who owned copies of these works, told his good friend Jesse W. Fell that he thought highly of Parker. Fell believed that Lincoln's religious views more closely resembled Parker's than those of any other theologian.

Lincoln may also have recalled the words that Galusha Grow, speaker of the U.S. House, uttered on July 4, 1861, the day Congress assembled for the first time after the bombardment of Fort Sumter: "Fourscore years ago fifty-six bold merchants, farmers, lawyers, and mechanics, the representatives of a few feeble colonists, scattered along the Atlantic seaboard, met in convention to found a new empire, based on the inalienable rights of man." Many newspapers published Grow's speech. (Both Grow and Lincoln were doubtless familiar with the Bible's statement about human longevity: "The days of our years are threescore years and ten.")

IN THIS NUMBERED SECTION, THE UNION SOLDIERS ARE COMPLETELY UNKNOWN, INCLUDING THEIR UNIT AND STATE.

Funny Graphic Gentlemen—A Day Long To Be Remembered

John Hay (1838-1905), who served as Lincoln's assistant private secretary from 1860 to 1865, kept an informative diary during the Civil War. Unfortunately, the entry describing events in Gettysburg on November 19, 1863, is frustratingly skimpy: "In the morning I got a beast and rode out with the President's suite to the Cemetery in the procession. The procession formed itself in an orphanly sort of way & moved out with very little help from anybody & after a little delay Mr. Everett took his place on the stand – And Mr. Stockton made a prayer which thought it was an oration – and Mr. Everett spoke as he always does perfectly – and the President in a firm free way, with more grace than is his wont said his half dozen words lines of consecration and the music wailed and we went home through crowded and cheering streets. And all the particulars are in the daily papers."

One such paper, the Washington, D.C., Daily Morning Chronicle, contained a long description of the day's events, dated November 19 and signed "J. H." It is almost certainly Hay's handiwork, though historians have failed to realize it. (An exception is Gabor Boritt, who acknowledged that Hay "may well have been the author.") It is well established that Hay wrote for that newspaper, which was widely regarded as the Lincoln Administration's organ. Its editor, John Wien Forney, told Hay in 1862: "I have taken some liberties with the MSS. which will not, I hope, be objected to." He added, "I am very anxious for your assistance, and earnestly ask you for it." A few months later, Hay wrote to his fellow White House secretary, John G. Nicolay: "I am getting apathetic & write blackguardly article for the Chronicle, from which West extracts the dirt & fun & publishes the dreary remains." The knowledgeable Washington correspondent for the Cincinnati Gazette, Whitelaw Reid, reported that Hay "is charged with occasional sparkling editorials in the Chronicle." Hay pasted some Daily Morning Chronicle editorials into a scrapbook of his own writings.

Following is John Hay's diary entry from the day the portrait on the adjacent page was made:

8 November 1863, Sunday

The President tells me that Meade is at last after the enemy and that Grant will attack tomorrow.

Went with Mrs Ames to Gardner's gallery & were soon joined by Nico[lay] & the Pres[iden]t. We had a great many pictures taken. Some of the Presdt. the best I have seen. Nico[lay] & I immortalized ourselves by having ourselves done in group with the Presdt.

In the evening Seward came in. . . .

This portrait of President Abraham Lincoln with his personal secretaries John G. Nicolay and John Hay was made by Alexander Gardner at his gallery in Washington, D.C., on Sunday, November 8, 1863, eleven days before the President delivered the Gettysburg Address. A detail of Lincoln is on page 123 from this image. (Lloyd Ostendorf collection)

During his years with Lincoln, Hay also contributed many anonymous and pseudonymous pieces to other newspapers, including two St. Louis papers (the Missouri <u>Democrat</u> and the Missouri <u>Republican</u>), the Providence, Rhode Island, <u>Journal</u>, the New York <u>World</u> (when it was a Republican paper), the Springfield <u>Illinois State Journal</u>, and the Washington <u>National Republican</u>. Occasionally he signed those pieces "J. H." just as he signed the article reproduced here.

While historians have often quoted from that piece, few have recognized it as Hay's authorship, and for good reason. The <u>Daily Morning Chronicle</u> published an article dated "Wednesday, [November] 18th," immediately before Hay's, which was dated "Thursday, November 19". The headline above the two pieces suggests that both were by the same author, but it seems clear that the first was by someone other than "J. H." Those initials appear at the end of the second dispatch but not the first. (The <u>Daily Morning Chronicle</u> deployed four correspondents at Gettysburg.) The style of the first article differs from that of the second, and Hay's diary indicates that he could not have been the author of the first article. The second article contains John Hay's literary fingerprints: unusual words ("clustering," a favorite of Hay's); use of an uncommon phrase in French, a language Hay knew (<u>coup d'oeil</u>); emphatic opinions; and shameless puns ("phonographic [i.e., stenographic] and funny graphic gentlemen"). Here is the text of that article:

The Day of the Dedication

Thursday, November 19

The sun never broke to life and warmth on a fairer fall day than this. A sharp night's frost was succeeded by one of the most beautiful Indian Summer days ever enjoyed. At an early hour, long before sunrise, the roads leading to Gettysburg were crowded by citizens from every quarter thronging into the village in every kind of vehicle—old Pennsylvania wagons, spring wagons, carts, family carriages, buggies, and more fashionable modern vehicles, all crowded with citizens—kept pouring into the town in one continual string, while the roads were constantly dotted with pedestrians by twos, by threes, singly, and in companies, all facing towards the village.

Thus the thronging in continued until late in the day, while the railroad disgorged its eager crowds, while the streets, ever filling, overflowed with the invading host.

Soon after breakfast I rode out to the Cemetery, and the crowds that I left in the town seemed to have duplicated themselves, and to have scattered all over the extensive area of the battle ground, wandering out to the seminary, strolling about the college, laboring to the summit of Round Top, examining Culp's Hill, tracing the plan of the Cemetery, seeking relics everywhere: the whole landscape was fairly studded with visitors, mostly on foot, many on horseback, and not a few in carriages, and, with maps in hand, getting up the field of battle, and realizing for the first time the grandeur and extent of the struggle about which they had heard so much.

Returning to the village, the scattered concourse we had left miles out in the country seemed to have got there before us, for the streets were full to overflowing, and yet they came.

The town was now enlivened by the procession forming and by the marshals and military. The various orders and delegations were being placed and arranged in the procession ready to set out.

At about 10 the President issued from Mr. Wills' house, and was greeted with three hearty cheers. Soon someone proclaimed three cheers for Father Abraham, and they were given with a will. Another call for three cheers for the next President of the United States was responded to with no less enthusiasm.

In the meanwhile the President had mounted, and was besieged by an eager crowd thronging around him, and anxious for the pleasure of taking him by the hand, while he sat pleasantly enjoying the hearty welcome thus spontaneously accorded, until the marshals, having mercy upon his oft-wrung arm and wearying exertions, caused the crowd to desist and allow the President to sit in peace upon his horse. But the people, not yet satisfied, must have another three cheers for honest Old Abe, and they fairly eclipsed all the others.

Mr. Lincoln appeared in black, with the usual crape bound around his hat in memory of his little son, and with white gauntlets upon his hands. The list of notables who were present is given in another column, and many of them mounted when he did, and they remained conversing together waiting for the moving of the procession.

Mr. Lincoln remarked upon the fair prospects spread out before him, and observed that he had expected to see more woods, an expectation, doubtless, that had been entertained by many besides himself.

In the meanwhile the throng of swaying, eager people, more remote from him, were crowding and jostling, ever restlessly trying to get a glimpse of Mr. Lincoln, many of whom, doubtless, saw for the first time a live President of the United States.

When the procession began to move I hastened to the platform, and arrived there long before the cavalcade appeared upon the ground. Taking our seat among the reporters, we endeavored to prepare ourselves to enable the readers of THE CHRONICLE to obtain some idea of the day's proceedings.

At about 11:20, the President arrived upon the platform, accompanied by Secretaries Seward, Blair, and Usher. Soon Governor Tod and Governor Brough came near, and Mr. Tod, in a hearty, cordial manner, said: "Mr. President, I want you to shake hands with me;" and Mr. Lincoln as cordially responded. He then introduced Governor Brough to the President, and also to Mr. Seward, who said, "Why, I have just seen Governor Dennison, of Ohio, and here are two more Governors of Ohio—how many more Governors has Ohio?" "She has only one more, sir," said Governor Brough, "and he's across the water."

By-and-by, Governor Tod said he had called on Governor Seward, but had not found him at home; also, on Mr. Usher: "Yes, sir," said Seward, "I visited the ground around the Seminary this morning, and Mr. Lincoln joined in. Well, Governor, you seem to have been to the State Department and to the Interior, I will now go with you to the Post Office Department;" whereupon he turned to Secretary Blair and introduced Governors Brough and Tod to him.

The crowd upon the ground were kept in the form of a hollow square, within which, while these things were proceeding, the procession had filed and the various companies forming it had taken up a position around the platform, while those who had tickets took their seats upon it.

We noticed delegations from Baltimore, Washington, and Philadelphia, and from the Masons, Odd-Fellows, Templars, and many of the Sons of Malta, who were not in regalia. The Sanitary Commission, too, were there, conspicuous by their banner, and precious by the memory of their extended usefulness and valuable services. Many States, too, were represented, and flags and banners enlivened the scene.

Five or six bands were also present, among which were the Marine band, of Washington, Birgfeld's band, the band of the 2d Regulars, from Fort McHenry, New York regimental band, and others.

At twenty minutes to twelve, Hon. Edward Everett arrived, and after being introduced to the President, the exercises at once proceeded. Marshal Lamon first announced that a letter had just been received from General Scott, regretting that his increasing infirmities rendered him unable to be present upon the occasion.

Birgfeld's band then played an introductory dirge, solemn and suitable for the occasion. The Rev. Thomas H. Stockton then offered a very impressive prayer. This was followed by Birgfeld's band, who gave us the Old Hundred in all its grand and sublime beauty—after which the Hon. Edward Everett was introduced by Marshal Lamon. Some idiot in the crowd at once proposed three cheers for Everett, which the good sense of the people immediately decided so irreverent upon such an occasion that no one responded, and Mr. Idiot subsided.

At this time the *coup d'oeil* of the scene was truly grand. Crowds of citizens surrounded the stand and stretched away into the distance, far out of any possible range of hearing. Many were in mourning, and the upturned tearful eyes of those who were near, indicated too plainly that to them the dedication was a sad pilgrimage also. Military officers and marshals on horseback, scattered through the crowd, added a pleasing variety to the scene; while the various regimental bands, societies in their regalia, and the bright and gay uniforms of officers and marshals, the banners, flags, and devices of the various regiments, associations, and delegations, all contributed to produce a blending and contrast of colors highly pleasing to behold.

Around, far off, scattered over the landscape, were crowds of people who, despairing of a near approach to the stand, the centre of interest, were satisfying their curiosity and enjoying the scene apparently apart from it. Below lay

Gettysburg, deserted and flag-bedecked, behind it the seminary and college, with their clustering historical associations; stretching before and beyond was the beautiful battlefield, now giving rich promise, as it had yielded past evidence of its abundant fertility. On the one side Culp's Hill, now precious in history, and on the other, far back in the distance, and surmounted by our beautiful flag, was the victory-crowned summit of Round Top. Far, far off, in distinct outline, were the South Mountains, forming a well defined frame to the whole picture. Minute guns added their impressiveness to the scene, while a daguerreotypist, with his instrument prominently placed at the outskirts of the main crowd, by the aid of the softly-glowing, hazy sun, endeavors to snatch and forever preserve the animated foreground, rich in eminent citizens.

Prominent in that foreground must not be omitted a beautiful in memoriam banner, born by a delegation of the Army of the Potomac, from the hospital at York, of which they, who had been wounded at Gettysburg, were yet inmates. This banner was in the deepest mourning. Upon it was an urn and an inscription: "Honor to our brave comrades." Upon the other side was, "In memory of those who fell at Gettysburg, July 1st, 2d, and 3d, 1863."

Mr. Everett spoke for about two hours, and his oration, fully reported elsewhere, need not be here produced. Those who read it will find that he did ample justice to his former celebrity, and to the impressive occasion.

After the oration the Baltimore Union Glee Club sung in a very beautiful style. A poem, by B. B. French, inspired and written upon the battlefield, was then delivered. The following is the poem:

Gettysburg

By B. B. FRENCH

'Tis holy ground—

This spot, where, in their graves,

We place our country's braves,

Who fell in Freedom's holy cause

Fighting for Liberties and Laws—

Let tears abound.

Here let them rest—

And summer's heat and winter's cold

Shall glow and freeze above this mould—

A thousand years shall pass away—

A Nation still shall mourn this clay,
Which now is blest.

Here, where they fell,
Oft shall the widow's tear be shed,
Oft shall fond parents mourn their dead,
The orphan here shall kneel and weep,
And maidens, where their lovers sleep,
Their woes shall tell.

Great God in Heaven!
Shall all this sacred blood be shed—
Shall we thus mourn our glorious dead,
Oh, shall the end be wrath and woe,
The knell of Freedom's overthrow—
A Country riven?

It will not be!
We trust, Oh God, Thy gracious power
To aid us in our darkest hour.
This be our prayer—"Oh Father! save
A people's Freedom from its grave—
All praise to Thee!"

The President then delivered his address, which, though short, glittered with gems, evincing the gentleness and goodness of heart peculiar to him, and will receive the attention and command the admiration of all of the tens of thousands who will read it.

It seemed to us that the President sensibly felt the solemnity of the occasion, and controlled himself by an effort. This might have been fancy, but it was our impression; and as such we record it.

The brief address of the President was followed by the dirge selected for the occasion—one of Percival's—sung by a choir mainly composed of Gettysburg ladies, and accompanied by Birgfeld's band.

After this, a benediction was pronounced by Rev. Dr. —— —, the President, we believe, of the College. Marshal Lamon then announced that at half-past four the Hon. Chas. Anderson, Lieutenant Governor elect of Ohio, would deliver an address at the Presbyterian church, which the President, his Cabinet, and the people, were invited to attend; he then proclaimed the assemblage dismissed, and while the procession was reforming, a battery of the 5th regulars fired a salvo of eight rounds from their four guns.

The Marine Band, of Washington, escorted the procession back to the town, and afterwards, with other bands alternating, kept the air resonant with melody until sunset.

Previous to the address of the Hon. C. Anderson, Gov. Seymour presented a flag to a New York regiment, and made an appropriate speech.

We are also informed that just as the President was going to hear Mr. Anderson, a gentleman introduced to him old John Burns, the soldier of 1812, and the only man in Gettysburg who volunteered to defend it; and that the President invited him to go with him and Secretary Seward to hear the speech, and, each taking his arm, the old man between the two great statesmen for whom he had literally fought and bled, was escorted by them to the church, where he sat between them during the speaking. This little incident must have been a truly gratifying compliment to the brave old hero.

This we did not witness, as we were at the railroad endeavoring to get homewards. Nobody seemed to know anything of the arrangements, and thousands were patiently waiting to get home.

It appeared finally that the directors of the road or some other power had ordered that no train should leave until after the President's special train had gone, and hence, although the time for the regular train was 1 o'clock, and hundreds literally had thronged to the depot to go by that, yet they and additional expectants, until the accumulating hundreds had swelled to thousands, were all compelled to wait until near 7 o'clock, six mortal, long, wearying, slowly-dragging hours. We are confident that our excellent President was not a party to this shameful mismanagement, and that had he known that so dense a crowd of citizens were waiting upon his movements he would not have delayed another minute—but it was, nevertheless, the case, that while at least two full and heavy trains might have been run to Hanover Junction and back between 1 and half-past 5, P.M., yet one of the largest crowds that ever waited at a depot were detained here through a most unfortunate mistake. To the credit of our citizens be it said they bore their delay with remarkable patience, and the Baltimore Union Glee Club relieved the weariness of a very large portion by singing in a superior manner a constant succession of patriotic and popular songs.

It was my good fortune to return at last on the President's special train, conducted to Baltimore by Mr. John

Vandanskee, who certainly deserved the thanks of many of the phonographic and funny graphic gentlemen on the train; for he courteously procured and fixed for them, at considerable trouble, an excellent light, around which, busy as bees, they compared notes and transcribed their phonographic reports for the papers for which they were laboring. Though neither a phono or funny grapher, he certainly obtained the thanks of your present correspondent.

The whole affair passed off admirably, saving the annoying and unnecessary railroad delays. There seemed an abundance to eat and drink; the crowd were of the best class of our American citizens, highly intelligent, refined, and of course quiet and orderly.

There seemed to me to be no sensible jar or discord to the whole proceedings. It struck me, however, that the flags upon the flagstaffs should have been at half-mast, and all should have been draped in black, especially those at Round Top and on the ground immediately in front of the platform. It appeared to me, too, that minute guns should have been fired from Round Top and Culp's Hill—at least from 9 until 4—throughout the day. Further than this there appeared nothing left undone that ought to have been done, and possibly there may exist ample reasons why the omissions I have indicated were permitted.

The train arrived at Washington at ten minutes to one on Friday morning, and thus ended the dedication of the Gettysburg Cemetery—a day long to be remembered by the Gettysburghers in this to them eventful year, and one whose effects will pass into history.

J.H.

A full moon sets in the twilight of dawn at the Evergreen Cemetery Gatehouse.

Hon. James C. Conkling
        My Dear Sir.

        Your letter inviting me to attend a mass-meeting of unconditional Union-men, to be held at the Capital of Illinois, on the 3d day of September, has been received.

        It would be very agreeable to me, to thus meet my old friends, at my own home; but I can not, just now, be absent from here, so long as a visit there, would require.

        The meeting is to be of all those who maintain unconditional devotion to the Union; and I am sure my old political friends will thank me for tendering, as I do, the nation's gratitude to those other noble men, whom no partizan malice, or partizan hope, can make false to the nation's life.

        There are those who are dissatisfied with me. To such I would say: You desire peace; and you blame me that we do not have it. But how can we attain it? There are but three conceivable ways. First, to suppress the rebellion by force of arms. This, I am trying to do.

        Are you for it? If you are, so far we are agreed. If you are not for it, a second way is, to give up the Union. I am against this. Are you for it? If you are, you should say so plainly. If you are not for force, nor yet for dissolution, there only remains some imaginable compromise. I do not believe any compromise, embracing the maintenance of the Union, is now possible. All I learn, leads to a directly opposite belief. The strength of the rebellion, is its military — its army. That army dominates all the country, and all the people, within its range. Any offer of terms made by any man or men within that range, in opposition to that army, is simply nothing for the present; because such man or men, have no power whatever to enforce their side of a compromise, if one were made with them. To illustrate — Suppose refugees from the South, and peace men of the North, get together in convention, and frame and proclaim a compromise embracing a restoration of the Union; in what way can that compromise be used to keep Lee's army out of Pennsylvania? Meade's army can keep Lee's army out of Pennsylvania; and, I think, can ultimately drive it out of existence. But no paper compromise, to which the controllers of Lee's army are not agreed, can, at all, affect that army....

...It is hard to say that anything has been more bravely, and well done, than at Antietam, Murfreesboro, Gettysburg, and on many fields of lesser note. Nor must Uncle Sam's Web-feet be forgotten. At all the watery margins they have been present. Not only on the deep sea, the broad bay, and the rapid river, but also up the narrow muddy bayou, and wherever the ground was a little damp, they have been, and made their tracks. Thanks to all. For the great republic—for the principle it lives by, and keeps alive— for man's vast future,— thanks to all.

Peace does not appear so distant as it did. I hope it will come soon, and come to stay; and so come as to be worth the keeping in all future time. It will then have been proved that, among free men, there can be no successful appeal from the ballot to the bullet; and that they who take such appeal are sure to lose their case, and pay the cost. And then, there will be some black men who can remember that, with silent tongue, and clenched teeth, and steady eye, and well-poised bayonet, they have helped mankind on to this great consummation; while, I fear, there will be some white ones, unable to forget that, with malignant heart, and deceitful speech, they have strove to hinder it.

Still let us not be over-sanguine of a speedy final triumph. Let us be quite sober. Let us diligently apply the means, never doubting that a just God, in his own good time, will give us the rightful result.

Yours very truly

A. Lincoln

LETTER TO JAMES C. CONKLING, SPRINGFIELD, ILLINOIS, AUGUST 26, 1863

THE PRESENT TEXT FOLLOWS THE LETTER SENT TO CONKLING, WHICH WAS COPIED BY A CLERK FROM THE FINAL DRAFT AND CORRECTED AND SIGNED BY LINCOLN. AN INSERTION SENT LATER BY TELEGRAPH AND SIGNIFICANT DELETIONS AND EMENDATIONS IN THE PRELIMINARY AND FINAL DRAFTS ARE INDICATED IN THE SUCCEEDING FOOTNOTES (OF THE COLLECTED WORKS).

they here, gave the l
votion — that we here
dead shall not hav
the nation, shall ha
dom, and that govern
the people for the p
ish from the earth

full measure of de=

highly resolve there

dead in vain; that

a new birth of free-

ment of the people by

ople, shall not per-

PAGE 189: AN 1875 MAP PUBLISHED IN PARIS AS PART OF A MILITARY ATLAS ON THE CIVIL WAR.
(DAVID RUMSEY MAP COLLECTION)

PAGES 193 & 194: A MAP PRODUCED IN 1863 BY JOHN BACHELDER SHOWING TROOP POSITIONS, ENDORSED BY GENERAL MEADE.
(LIBRARY OF CONGRESS COLLECTION)

PAGE 196: AN 1895 MAP PRODUCED BY THE WAR DEPARTMENT AS PART OF A MILITARY ATLAS.
(DAVID RUMSEY MAP COLLECTION)

PAGE 190 & ABOVE: THE EVERGREEN CEMETERY GATEHOUSE WAS A FAVORITE SUBJECT OF PHOTOGRAPHERS FOLLOWING THE EPIC BATTLE. THESE SIMILAR PHOTOGRAPHS OF THE GATEHOUSE WERE MADE BY BRADY & CO. APPROXIMATELY TWO WEEKS AFTER THE BATTLE. THE IMAGES OBVIOUSLY WERE NOT MADE AT THE SAME TIME, BUT WERE MADE ON THE SAME TRIP TO GETTYSBURG. AT THE TIME OF THE BATTLE, ELIZABETH THORN WAS CARETAKER OF EVERGREEN CEMETERY. SHE LIVED HERE WITH HER FAMILY, LATER WRITING A VIVID ACCOUNT OF HER EXPERIENCE. HERE HUSBAND PETER WAS SERVING IN THE UNION ARMY AT A DIFFERENT LOCATION. (LIBRARY OF CONGRESS COLLECTION)

1.

EXPLANATION OF CHARACTERS USED.

Stone Wall, Virginia Fence.
Straight Fence (rail or board).
Pine, Oak, Round Leaf.
House, Church, Outbuilding.

Union Works.
House Burned.
Signal Station.

The plane of reference for the horizontal curves is taken 30 ft. below a bench mark on Cemetery Hill. Distance between curves, 20 feet.

Summits and lowest points are marked with their appropriate references.

The figures in the bed of Rock Creek indicate the ordinary low water stage, and it is fordable for all arms at most all places. The other creeks are similar in depth and are also fordable, the contours showing in all cases where the banks are too precipitous. All are subject to sudden rises, sometimes as great as 10 ft. above the present level.

At places where there are two names, the upper one gives the resident at the time of the survey in 1868-9. On the authority of Mr. J. B. Bachelder, the lower names are of residents at the time of the battle. The map was revised on the ground by P. M. Blake, C. E., in May and June, 1869, and the additions and corrections indicated show the positions of fences, buildings, etc., at time of battle. Buildings marked with a cross were not standing at time of battle. The letters near buildings show the material of which the latter are made, thus: B, brick; W, wood; S. stone.

The top of this map is North.

ENGINEER DEPARTMENT, U.S.A.
BVT. MAJ. GEN. A. A. HUMPHREYS, Brig. Gen. and Chief of Engineers.

MAP OF THE
BATTLE-FIELD of GETTYSBURG.
Surveyed and drawn under the direction of BVT. MAJ. GEN. G.K.WARREN, Maj. of Engineers.

by 1st Lieut. W.H.CHASE, Corps of Engineers,
assisted by 1st Lieut. THOMAS TURTLE, Corps of Engineers,
2d Lieut. F.A.HINMAN, Corps of Engineers,
and CIVIL ASSISTANTS

Capt. C.E.DAVIS (Topography) | Gen. H.A.FRINK (Levels) | W.F.HILL (Levels)
JOHN H. DAGER (Topography) | EDWIN A. CHASE (Topography) | E.C.MORRISON (Levels)
DRAUGHTSMEN: Edwin A. Chase, W. A. Wansleben, John H. Dager, C. F. Trill.

Scale
0   500   1000   1500   2000   2500 Feet

Official

NOTE.
This Survey was made during part of the Fall of 1868 and during the Summer and Fall of 1869 (Oct. 21st, 1868–Oct. 23d, 1869). The parties of 1869 were composed of Engineer Soldiers detailed from the Battalion for that purpose.
Numerous changes have occurred since the Battle, in direction of fences, new roads being opened, houses erected, woods cleared, etc.

GETTYSBURG

The annual Remembrance Illumination at the Soldiers' National Cemetery during
the Dedication Day and Remembrance Day tribute to the fallen soldiers at Gettysburg.

Telling the Story

The story of Lincoln in Gettysburg is unique in history. The events in 1863 are compelling and fascinating. It is a true story from beginning to end. There is no need to exaggerate or embellish any of this legend. The Battle of Gettysburg was the largest battle on the American continent, consuming a town and its people. It led to the creation of the first national cemetery on a battlefield and culminated in a visit by President Abraham Lincoln who delivered there what has become a timeless monument to revered ideals. And the event was photographed.

It seems odd to include this last point, but events were rarely photographed at the time. Illustrated magazines were the primary source for visual images depicting people, locations, and events. Photography was still a new technology and had only been used outside of portraiture for a few years. Photographing moving people and objects was difficult to accomplish. With six- and seven-second exposures for cameras, even small movements were blurred. The equipment was cumbersome and the delicate glass plates required rigorous on-site chemical processing.

The Civil War was the fourth war to be captured with the lens, but the first war to be photographed extensively. The four-year national crisis created a compelling subject for the evolution of photojournalism. There are believed to be approximately ten to twenty thousand documentary photographs from the Civil War that still exist. The original number of documentary photographs created during the war far exceeded this, but after the war was over, most photographs were discarded or the glass plates sold. The country was sick of war and didn't want to look at it anymore. (This estimate of the number of photographs made does not include hundreds of thousands of portraits made of soldiers.)

We are fortunate to have a small collection of images from November 19, 1863, thanks to several diligent photographers who knew history was being made (though they could never have fully imagined their value). There were probably many more photographs from the day made originally, but only a small group have survived. These surviving images help to tell the story. They are special, revealing intrinsic qualities about the people that seem very familiar, as though they could have been taken a week ago, but other aspects that seem foreign, as from a time long ago.

Telling the story of Lincoln in Gettysburg is much larger than the two days in November, 1863, that are the heart of this legend. To tell the whole story, we must look at the events leading up to

THE "ONE GREAT BATTLE," AS LINCOLN DESCRIBED IT. THE EPIC BEGINS WITH THE CONFEDERATE ARMY IMMINENTLY THREATENING INVASION OF THE NORTH AND PENNSYLVANIA'S UNDERSTANDABLE REACTION TO THE REBEL ARMY COMING THEIR DIRECTION. THE STORY CONTINUES WITH LINCOLN'S STRUGGLE TO CONVINCE GENERAL HOOKER TO EFFECTIVELY COOPERATE WITH GENERAL-IN-CHIEF HALLECK AS THE REBELS MOVED UP THE SHENANDOAH VALLEY INTO THE CUMBERLAND VALLEY WEST OF SOUTH MOUNTAIN.

ON THE FIRST DAY OF JULY, THE GIANT BATTLE BEGAN. THE UNTHINKABLE UNFOLDED. TIME STOOD STILL IN GETTYSBURG FOR THREE DAYS. MISERY SHROUDED THE THOUSANDS OF WOUNDED, HUNDREDS WHO REMAINED FOR WEEKS OR MONTHS IN FIELD HOSPITALS. FOR THE INHABITANTS OF THE TOWN AND SURROUNDING AREA, LIFE WOULD NEVER BE THE SAME. THE COUNTRY WAS AGAIN SHOCKED, BUT FOR THE NORTH, THE NEWS OF A VICTORY AND LEE ON THE RUN WAS WELCOME NEWS.

THE STORY CONTINUES WITH LINCOLN'S FRUSTRATION AND DISTRESS IN MOTIVATING GENERAL MEADE TO FINISH WHAT HE STARTED AT GETTYSBURG. THE PRESIDENT POLITELY, BUT FIRMLY TRIED TO IMPEL MEADE TO TAKE DECISIVE ACTION TO DESTROY THE REBEL ARMY WHILE THEY WERE IN THE NORTH. GENERAL MEADE AND HIS STAFF FAILED TO DEVISE AND EXECUTE A PLAN TO CRUSH, OR EVEN IMPAIR LEE'S EXHAUSTED ARMY. MEADE MADE LITTLE EFFORT TO TRY AND HOLD THE RETREATING CONFEDERATES AT THE POTOMAC, AN ARMY THAT CERTAINLY HAD DWINDLING SUPPLIES. THE BUNGLE INFURIATED LINCOLN, AS HE HAD ENDURED INCOMPETENCE REPEATEDLY FOR TWO YEARS BEFORE GETTYSBURG.

THE GETTYSBURG STORY GRADUALLY IMPROVES IN THE AFTERMATH OF THE HORRENDOUS DEVASTATION. AFTER SEVERAL MONTHS, THE DESPERATE HEALTH CONDITIONS MENACING THE BOROUGH AND SURROUNDING REGION SLOWLY BEGAN TO RECOVER. THE FORESIGHT OF DAVID WILLS AND OTHER MEN CONCERNED ABOUT THEIR COMMUNITY, PENNSYLVANIA, AND THE OTHER STATES WHO LOST SOLDIERS, LED TO A BRIGHTER DAY WITH THE PLANS FOR A WELL-CONCEIVED NATIONAL CEMETERY. WHILE THE SITUATION IN GETTYSBURG IMPROVED, THE DEMANDS ON PRESIDENT LINCOLN WERE ENORMOUS.

1863 BEGAN TO TRANSFORM WITH THE SUCCESSES AT GETTYSBURG AND VICKSBURG. THE THIRD CRUCIAL VICTORY OF THE YEAR WOULD COME ONLY DAYS AFTER LINCOLN GAVE THE GETTYSBURG ADDRESS, WITH VICTORIES IN THE BATTLES OF CHATTANOOGA. BUT IN THE EARLY FALL OF THE YEAR, AS PLANS FOR THE NATIONAL CEMETERY DEVELOPED, THE UNION ARMY CLASHED WITH THE CONFEDERATES AT CHICKAMAUGA IN WHAT WAS THE SECOND-LARGEST BATTLE OF THE CIVIL WAR ON SEPTEMBER 19 AND 20, 1863. SOON AFTER THIS GIANT UNION OFFENSIVE, IN OCTOBER, THE CHATTANOOGA CAMPAIGN DEVELOPED WHEN LINCOLN PUT GENERAL ULYSSES S. GRANT IN COMMAND OF THE ENTIRE WESTERN WAR FRONT, EXCEPT FOR LOUISIANA. A SERIES OF IMPORTANT UNION VICTORIES

SET THE STAGE FOR THRUSTING ATTACKS TOWARD ATLANTA. ULTIMATELY, IT WAS THE BATTLES OF THE ATLANTA CAMPAIGN AND THE CITY'S SURRENDER WHICH INSURED LINCOLN'S REELECTION THE FOLLOWING YEAR AND THE END OF THE WAR WITH THE UNION INTACT.

THE CLIMAX OF THE STORY OF LINCOLN IN GETTYSBURG BEGINS WITH THE REQUEST FOR PRESIDENT LINCOLN TO SPEAK AT THE DEDICATION OF THE SOLDIERS' NATIONAL CEMETERY, OFTEN REFERRED TO IN 1863 AS THE CONSECRATION OF THE NATIONAL CEMETERY AT GETTYSBURG. BY SOMETIME IN OCTOBER, LINCOLN BECAME AWARE HE WOULD BE INVITED TO GIVE A SPEECH, CONSECRATING THE NEW CEMETERY. HE RECEIVED A LETTER FROM DAVID WILLS OFFICIALLY INVITING HIM TO SPEAK ABOUT TWO WEEKS BEFORE THE NOVEMBER CEREMONY. LINCOLN SAW THE DEDICATION AS AN IMPORTANT OPPORTUNITY TO COMMUNICATE A MESSAGE TO THE COUNTRY. HE KNEW A SPEECH FROM GETTYSBURG WOULD BE WIDELY PRINTED IN NEWSPAPERS THROUGHOUT THE COUNTRY AND THAT A SHORT SPEECH WOULD BE READ BY MILLIONS. IN THE DAYS BEFORE PRESS SECRETARIES, PRESS CONFERENCES, WEB SITES, AND MAILING LISTS, LINCOLN CONVEYED INFORMATION TO THE PUBLIC THROUGH NEWSPAPERS. NEWSPAPER ARTICLES WERE THE INSTRUMENT HE COULD USE TO COMMUNICATE HIS BELIEFS AND HIS POSITION ON ISSUES.

PRESIDENT LINCOLN BEGAN TO COMPOSE HIS MESSAGE. THE SUBSTANCE OF LINCOLN'S ADDRESS WAS NOTHING NEW. HE ALREADY KNEW EXACTLY WHAT HE WANTED TO SAY, BUT HE NEEDED TO ARTICULATE THE MESSAGE CLEARLY AND ELEGANTLY TO HIS LISTENERS, AND HIS READERS. THE CENTRAL THEME AND BEGINNING OF HIS MESSAGE, "ALL MEN ARE CREATED EQUAL", WAS PRESENTED IN HIS FAMOUS PEORIA SPEECH ON OCTOBER 16, 1854, BUT LIKELY IN A SPEECH IN SPRINGFIELD PRIOR TO THAT. HE REITERATED THIS BELIEF NUMEROUS TIMES THROUGHOUT ILLINOIS, INCLUDING THE LINCOLN-DOUGLAS DEBATES. EVEN LINCOLN'S OPENING LINE IN THE ADDRESS, REFERRING TO THE TIME FRAME, HAS A SIMILAR CONNECTION TO THE PEORIA SPEECH.

PRESIDENT LINCOLN KNEW THE REASON HE WAS GOING TO GETTYSBURG—HE ALWAYS SINCERELY REMEMBERED THE SOLDIERS. HIS EXPRESSION OF GRATITUDE AND HONOR TOWARD THE SOLDIERS IS ENDEARING AND POIGNANT. IT IS NO WONDER THAT LINCOLN'S WORDS WERE CHOSEN TO BE ENGRAVED ON MONUMENTS IN THE CEMETERY AND ON THE BATTLEFIELD AFTER THE WAR.

WE KNOW THAT LINCOLN CONSIDERED THE DEDICATION AND HIS ADDRESS VERY IMPORTANT. LINCOLN TOLD SECRETARY STANTON TO CHANGE THE ORIGINAL TRAVEL PLANS. HE WANTED THE TRIP TO BE TWO DAYS INSTEAD OF ONE IN ORDER TO AVOID ANY CHANCE OF A DELAY.

ELEVEN DAYS BEFORE THE EVENT, THE PRESIDENT WENT TO ALEXANDER GARDNER'S WASHINGTON, D.C. GALLERY FOR A PORTRAIT SESSION. THE SITTING APPEARS TO HAVE BEEN A LONGER-THAN-NORMAL PORTRAIT SESSION, WITH AT LEAST FIVE PORTRAITS MADE, PROBABLY MORE. IT IS POSSIBLY THE LARGEST PORTRAIT SESSION LINCOLN EVER DID.

Sittings for someone prominent during the mid-1800's were usually two to four photographs. Was it a coincidence that so many photographs were taken, or did Lincoln (and Gardner) believe he was getting ready to do something big? Alexander Gardner also went to Gettysburg to photograph for stereoviews.

The greatest evidence of the importance Lincoln placed on going to Gettysburg was the degree of meticulous care in which he thoroughly fine-tuned his words. Lincoln perfected each line and word with precision, like a great composer would a fine piece of music. Lincoln sought Secretary Seward's input, as he had often done and valued his close friend's recommendations, and that is more evidence of its importance. He started writing the speech in Washington, worked on it off and on for days prior to the dedication as time would allow, and completed a copy prior to leaving Washington on November 18. It is obvious he continued to analyze every possible perception of it, shaping every word. We will probably never answer all the questions regarding the Gettysburg Address. What happened to the reading copy? Did he write one or more new copies with subtle changes while at the Wills House that are lost? How many total copies were there?

Although this mystery will likely never be resolved, the story of the Nicolay copy seems to have a logical explanation. President Lincoln had apparently completed this copy on Executive Mansion letterhead while in his office. This is the copy that likely made the trip to Gettysburg, and while making final preparations at the Wills house, he rewrote the second page on foolscap, paper he probably received from David Wills or at his house. On the eve of the ceremony, and possibly the next morning, he most likely wrote a new copy that became the reading copy, which he probably gave to a reporter following the ceremony.

Two interesting parts of the story—while President Lincoln gave the address, he was said to be referencing his reading copy. This is understandable with the last-minute polishing. He didn't want to miss a single word—such as the late addition of "under God".

Second, on the day of dedication, friends and colleagues close to Lincoln observed how he also took special care in how he delivered the address. When he gave a speech, he was usually animated and often spoke with gestures. But, because it was a solemn occasion, the President wanted to be reserved and appear respectful at all times, so he moved very little.

Dedication Day was exciting for everyone who attended. Accounts tell us Lincoln enjoyed his two-day visit to the borough. He was given a warm welcome and was always the center of attention,

EXCEPT DURING MOST OF THE CEREMONY. THE DEDICATION CEREMONY HAD SEVERAL SPEAKERS, MIXED WITH MUSIC. ALTHOUGH A SOMBER OCCASION, THE TOWN AND VISITORS SEEMED TO VIEW THE EVENT WITH CELEBRATION BEFORE AND AFTER THE CEREMONY. EVERYONE WAS CERTAINLY EXCITED TO SEE THE PRESIDENT, AND AS JOHN HAY POINTED OUT, IT WAS PROBABLY THE FIRST TIME MOST PEOPLE HAD SEEN A PRESIDENT.

WHEN IT WAS TIME FOR LINCOLN TO DEPART GETTYSBURG, HIS ENTOURAGE WENT TO THE TRAIN STATION. A LARGE CROWD WAS WAITING FOR THE PRESIDENT'S TRAIN TO LEAVE FIRST, AND SOON EVERYONE WAS GOING HOME. NO ONE KNOWS WHEN HE BEGAN FEELING THE ONCOMING ILLNESS THAT WOULD PLAGUE HIM IN THE WEEKS THAT FOLLOWED. THE DAY AFTER THE DEDICATION, LINCOLN PENNED A LETTER IN THE EXECUTIVE MANSION DISPLAYING HIS USUAL WIT, EXCHANGED LETTERS WITH EDWARD EVERETT, AND PERFORMED SEVERAL DUTIES. ON NOVEMBER 21, THE VARIOLOID (A MILD FORM OF SMALLPOX) WORSENED AND LINCOLN WAS QUARANTINED FOR NEARLY THREE WEEKS. THE TIMING OF THE DEDICATION NARROWLY MISSED THIS ILLNESS THAT WOULD HAVE CERTAINLY PROHIBITED HIS TRAVEL.

WHILE WORKING ON THIS PROJECT AND LIVING IN GETTYSBURG SEVERAL MONTHS, ABSORBING THE PLACE IN AN ATTEMPT TO SUCCESSFULLY TELL THIS STORY, TWO THINGS STRUCK ME. FIRST, WHILE STUDYING THE AREA, I TOOK ADVANTAGE OF MANY OF THE EXCEPTIONAL TOURS AND PROGRAMS THE NATIONAL PARK SERVICE OFFERS. ON ONE TOUR IN THE CEMETERY, I HEARD THE PARK RANGER SAY THAT THE NUMBER ONE QUESTION HE IS ASKED AT THE PARK IS, "WHERE DID LINCOLN GIVE THE GETTYSBURG ADDRESS?" IT WASN'T A QUESTION RELATED TO THE BATTLE OR A QUESTION ABOUT SOMETHING SPECIFIC ON THE LARGE BATTLEFIELD, IT WAS ABOUT LINCOLN'S WORDS. A FEW WEEKS LATER, I HEARD A DIFFERENT PARK RANGER ON A TOUR SAY THE SAME THING. I FOUND IT VERY INTRIGUING AND IT STUCK WITH ME. I AM SURE THIS IS NOT TRUE FOR EVERY PARK RANGER, AND A DETAILED STUDY OF VISITORS MIGHT NOT YIELD THE SAME RESULTS, BUT THERE IS SOMETHING VERY INTERESTING ABOUT THIS.

WHY DOES THE GETTYSBURG ADDRESS STILL TOUCH SO MANY PEOPLE? WHAT INTRINSIC QUALITIES CONNECT SO MANY OF US TO IT? IS IT THE CENTRAL THEME OF THE ADDRESS ABOUT THE TRANSCENDENT PRINCIPLE OF EQUALITY THAT WILL ALWAYS BE A PREDOMINANT HUMAN NEED?

IS IT THE MOVING TRIBUTE TO THE SOLDIER'S SACRIFICE AND OUR OBLIGATION TO ALWAYS REMEMBER THEIR ABSOLUTE DEDICATION?

IS IT THE POWERFUL LAST LINE, "THAT GOVERNMENT OF THE PEOPLE, BY THE PEOPLE, FOR THE PEOPLE" THAT EXPRESSES THE DUTY OF CITIZENS, THE COUNTRY'S LEADERSHIP, AND THE GOVERNMENT? I THINK MANY PEOPLE CAN RELATE TO THIS WITH THE ONGOING FRUSTRATION WITH WASHINGTON POLITICS.

IS IT THE CLEAR MESSAGE "THAT THIS NATION, UNDER GOD"? LINCOLN DESCRIBING A COUNTRY WITH GOD'S

BLESSINGS AS HE OFTEN DID, CERTAINLY MEANS A GREAT DEAL TO MANY PEOPLE.

IS IT THE UNDERLYING THEME THAT FLOWS THROUGHOUT THE ENTIRE ADDRESS—THE IMPORTANCE OF DEDICATION TO COUNTRY?

ITS ATTRACTION IS PROBABLY DIFFERENT FOR EVERYBODY—IT IS MOST LIKELY SOME OR ALL OF THESE IDEALS. BUT IN THESE IDEALS, PEOPLE FEEL CONNECTED AND KNOW THEY ARE JUST AS RELEVANT TODAY AS THEY WERE WHEN LINCOLN FIRST WROTE THEM AND FOLDED UP THE SPEECH. WITH THE PROBLEMS FACING THE COUNTRY BOTH FROM OUTSIDE AND FROM WITHIN, WE CAN ALWAYS TURN TO LINCOLN AND THIS SUCCINCT, ELOQUENT SPEECH FOR GUIDANCE.

THE SECOND THING THAT STRUCK ME AFTER SPENDING A LOT OF TIME IN GETTYSBURG, WAS LINCOLN'S LARGE PRESENCE HERE. I HAVE ALWAYS LIVED IN THE HEART OF LINCOLN COUNTRY IN CENTRAL ILLINOIS, WHERE ABRAHAM LINCOLN LIVED, WORKED, AND FREQUENTLY TRAVELED FOR THIRTY YEARS. UNTIL COMING TO GETTYSBURG, I DIDN'T THINK THERE WAS ANOTHER PLACE WHERE LINCOLN'S PRESENCE WAS STILL CELEBRATED ON SUCH A LARGE SCALE, OUTSIDE OF WASHINGTON, D.C.

MOST OF US ENJOY CROSSING PATHS WITH HISTORY. TELLING THE STORY OF PRESIDENT ABRAHAM LINCOLN IN GETTYSBURG AND DISCOVERING THE STORY HAS BEEN AN ADVENTURE.

ROBERT SHAW, GETTYSBURG, JULY, 2013

... I am constantly pressed by those who scold before they think, or without thinking at all, ...

LETTER TO MAJOR GENERAL JOHN MCCLERNAND FROM THE EXECUTIVE MANSION, AUGUST 12, 1863

... I hope to "stand firm" enough to not go backward, and yet not go forward fast enough to wreck the country's cause.

LETTER TO ZACHARIAH CHANDLER FROM THE EXECUTIVE MANSION, THE DAY AFTER RETURNING FROM GETTYSBURG, NOVEMBER 20, 1863

... It is easy to see that, under the sharp discipline of civil war, the nation is beginning a new life. ...

ANNUAL MESSAGE TO CONGRESS, DECEMBER 8, 1863

Photographs from 1863

When we think of pictures taken during Lincoln's time, we think of black and white images. After the turn of the century, black and white images were printed on silver gelatin paper, which are the black and white prints we see today. But during the 1860s, prints were made using albumen paper. This was paper coated with egg whites and chloride, then floated in a silver nitrate bath. It could then be toned using a variety of mixtures, with gold toner being the most popular. Prints would take on a rich purplish-brown color. Frequently albumen prints viewed today have a yellowish cast, which is due to the aging process, and would not have been visible when new.

Two of the most popular forms of photography during this period were CDVs and stereoviews. CDVs, from the French carte-de-visite or visiting card, became the standard for portraits. An albumen print was pasted on a card measuring 2 ½" x 4". Local photographers would offer twelve CDVs for a dollar, that way you could keep one and pass the others around to friends and family. They became so popular that military leaders, politicians, actors, and other prominent people appeared on CDVs and were also collected. Special albums, with pockets on the pages, were made in order to hold the CDVs. The modern photo album evolved from this.

A stereoview consisted of two prints, each with a different perspective, pasted side by side on a card. Viewed through a stereoscope they formed a realistic 3-D image. They were a popular form of entertainment; every topic imaginable was photographed in stereo. The majority of outdoor Civil War photographs were taken in this fashion. Newspapers of the day couldn't reproduce photographs, only woodcuts. It was through the stereoviews taken at Antietam, Gettysburg, and other battlefields, that the public got their first realistic look at the true horror of war.

Some of the historic images used in this book were made from original stereo and CDV negatives. If the negative was no longer available, then a contact print was used. All were restored to resemble how they looked when new.

John J. Richter, Pages 204 & 205
Director of Imaging, The Center For Civil War Photography

Co-Author of Lincoln in 3-D published by Chronicle Books, Gettysburg in 3-D
and Antietam in 3-D published by The Center For Civil War Photography

To learn more about photography from the Civil War, contact The Center For Civil War Photography. For information on membership, seminars, books, and other upcoming programs, visit their website: www.civilwarphotography.org

PHOTOGRAPHERS AT THE DEDICATION

DAVID BACHRACH JR., BALTIMORE, MARYLAND, PHOTOGRAPHER

ONLY EIGHTEEN AT THE TIME, DAVID BACHRACH JR. WAS ON A PLATFORM ABOUT NINETY FEET AWAY FROM THE SPEAKER'S STAND. HE RECALLED IN AN INTERVIEW FIFTY-THREE YEARS LATER THAT HE WAS PHOTOGRAPHING THE SCENE FOR HARPER'S WEEKLY, AN ILLUSTRATED NEWSPAPER. WHEN HE FINISHED, HE TURNED THE NEGATIVES OVER TO THEM FOR THE WOODCUT ARTISTS TO USE IN MAKING THE DRAWINGS FOR THE PAPER.

HE PHOTOGRAPHED ONE KNOWN PLATE VIEW OF THE DEDICATION FROM A TEMPORARY PLATFORM.

ALEXANDER GARDNER, WASHINGTON D.C., PHOTOGRAPHER

SCOTTISH-BORN, ALEXANDER GARDNER MANAGED MATHEW B. BRADY'S WASHINGTON GALLERY. DURING THE CIVIL WAR, HE WAS THE FIRST PHOTOGRAPHER TO PHOTOGRAPH THE DEAD AT ANTIETAM, AND ALSO PRESIDENT LINCOLN'S VISIT TO THE BATTLEFIELD. HE ESTABLISHED HIS OWN WASHINGTON D.C. GALLERY IN 1863. HE ARRIVED AT GETTYSBURG WITHIN DAYS OF THE BATTLE AND PHOTOGRAPHED THE DEAD. HE WAS THE ONLY PHOTOGRAPHER TO PHOTOGRAPH THE LINCOLN CONSPIRATORS AND THEIR EXECUTION BY HANGING. AFTER THE WAR HE PUBLISHED A TWO-VOLUME SET, GARDNER'S PHOTOGRAPHIC SKETCH BOOK OF THE WAR, CONTAINING ONE HUNDRED HAND-PRINTED VIEWS PASTED ON EACH PAGE.

HE PHOTOGRAPHED THREE KNOWN STEREOS FROM AN ELEVATED POSITION DURING THE DEDICATION.

TYSON BROTHERS (CHARLES & ISAAC), GETTYSBURG, PENNSYLVANIA, PHOTOGRAPHERS

CHARLES AND ISAAC OPENED THEIR FIRST GETTYSBURG GALLERY IN 1859. IN 1863, WITHIN WEEKS OF THE BATTLE, THEY PHOTOGRAPHED A SERIES OF PLATE VIEWS SHOWING POINTS OF INTEREST ON THE BATTLEFIELD. BY 1866, CHARLES HAD SOLE OWNERSHIP, AND IN 1867 OFFERED A SERIES OF 80 STEREOVIEWS OF THE BATTLEFIELD.

THEY PHOTOGRAPHED THREE KNOWN PLATE VIEWS OF THE PROCESSION ON BALTIMORE STREET, WHICH PRECEDED THE DEDICATION.

PETER S. WEAVER, HANOVER, PENNSYLVANIA, PHOTOGRAPHER

PETER'S FATHER SAMUEL WAS AN EARLY PHOTOGRAPHER IN GETTYSBURG. PETER OPENED HIS FIRST GALLERY IN HANOVER IN 1861. HE PHOTOGRAPHED MANY SCENES AROUND GETTYSBURG IN OCTOBER AND NOVEMBER 1863. IN 1867, PETER TEAMED UP WITH HIS COUSIN, HANSON E. WEAVER, TO PRODUCE A SERIES OF STEREOVIEWS "GEMS AROUND THE BATTLE FIELD OF GETTYSBURG".

HE PHOTOGRAPHED TWO KNOWN PLATE VIEWS OF THE DEDICATION.

Photographs from 2013

The objective of this new collection of photographs in <u>A Day Long To Be Remembered</u> was to create images that would take readers back in time and to accurately depict scenes by using only photographic techniques. The new photographs were made in Gettysburg over a two-year period. After researching and studying locations for several weeks, the creation of images culminated into four months of 24/7 photography.

The first consideration was to create all the images near the actual dates the events originally occurred. I wanted the trees, color in the leaves, light and shadows, and the location of the rising and setting sun to all be accurate to the actual dates. I worked from the end of June, through all of July, to early August for the battlefield photographs, and for some images from the cemetery. Most battlefield photographs that are part of the final selection for the book where taken in the first two weeks of July.

The photographs telling the story of Lincoln's visit had to be made in the autumn and late autumn. Lincoln was in Gettysburg November 18 and 19, the day being described as a beautiful autumn day. Study of the procession photographs reveals some trees still had their leaves, while others had lost all their leaves. This was true on the dates November 18 and 19 while I worked there—some trees had all their leaves, while many other trees were bare. The other consideration on this subject is that photographing all bare trees looks like winter. So photography had to be started early, because every autumn is different and trees turn at different times each year.

One of my favorite photographs in the book is of the Gettysburg Presbyterian Church at twilight because I was able to make a good photograph at the exact same date and time Lincoln was there. I had photographed the church at other times earlier, but the best image came on November 19, late in the afternoon.

In presenting photographs that successfully take viewers back to 1863, other considerations had to be made. I wanted to create images that captured the essence of the place and event. In the battlefield photographs, I wanted images that felt like war (which is hard to do when you're missing thousands of soldiers, horses, cannons, limbers, caissons, and wagons). The photographs could rarely be taken under blue skies. I had to keep most monuments out. I used early morning fog frequently because it best captures the appearance of thick smoke and the dark, gloomy atmosphere that would

PERMEATE THE LOOK OF REAL BATTLE. IT ALSO CONVEYS A PERCEPTION OF MYSTERY AND CONFUSION THAT ARE ALSO COMMONLY PART OF BATTLES.

WHILE TRYING TO ACHIEVE THE GOAL OF CREATING PHOTOGRAPHS THAT GIVE A SENSE OF WHAT A LOCATION ACTUALLY LOOKED LIKE IN 1863 (THE BEST THAT IS POSSIBLE CONSIDERING 150 YEARS HAVE PASSED), IT IS NECESSARY TO KEEP MODERN ELEMENTS OUT OF THE IMAGE. SIGNS, MODERN BUILDINGS, TOWERS, ELECTRICAL TRANSFORMERS, AND AUTOMOBILES HAVE TO BE KEPT OUT OR THE DISTRACTION RUINS A PHOTOGRAPH'S ABILITY TO CONNECT TO THE VIEWER.

GETTYSBURG WAS AN EXCITING PLACE TO UNDERTAKE A LARGE PHOTOGRAPHY PROJECT. IT IS A BEAUTIFUL TOWN AND LANDSCAPE WITH ROLLING HILLS, AND MOUNTAINS IN THE DISTANCE. THE NATIONAL PARK SERVICE AND GETTYSBURG FOUNDATION HAVE DONE AN OUTSTANDING JOB OF PRESERVING AND RESTORING THE BATTLEFIELD TO ITS ORIGINAL 1863 APPEARANCE.

ALL THE IMAGES IN THIS BOOK WERE MADE WITH NIKON DIGITAL SLR CAMERAS AND NIKKOR LENSES. THERE WAS NO COMPUTER MANIPULATION OF FOG, SKIES, MOONS, FLAGS, OR OTHER FEATURES IN THE PHOTOGRAPHS. TRIPODS WERE USED IN MAKING ALL PHOTOGRAPHS. THE PHOTOGRAPHS WERE MADE IN RAW FORMAT AND PROCESSED USING AN APPLE MAC PRO COMPUTER WITH A COLOR-CALIBRATED EIZO MONITOR.

CREDITS FOR 1863 PHOTOGRAPHS, DOCUMENTS, AND MAPS

PHOTOGRAPHS FROM 1863
PAGES 69, 70, 74, 123, 124, 175 LLOYD OSTENDORF COLLECTION
PAGE 96 ADAMS COUNTY HISTORICAL SOCIETY COLLECTION
PAGE 116 HANOVER AREA HISTORICAL SOCIETY COLLECTION
PAGE 8 INDIANA HISTORICAL SOCIETY COLLECTION
PAGES 105, 108, 109, 110, 135, 190 LIBRARY OF CONGRESS COLLECTION
PAGES 97, 98, 111 & 112, 113 & 114, 115 NATIONAL ARCHIVES AND RECORDS ADMINISTRATION COLLECTION

DOCUMENTS
PAGES 191 & 192 JOHN J. RICHTER COLLECTION
PAGE 99 GETTYSBURG NATIONAL MILITARY PARK MUSEUM COLLECTION
PAGES 120, 121 NATIONAL ARCHIVES AND RECORDS ADMINISTRATION COLLECTION
PAGES 6 & 7, 142 & 143, 186 & 187 LIBRARY OF CONGRESS COLLECTION, MANUSCRIPT DIVISION

MAPS
MAPS ON PAGES 1, 2, 36, 37, 189, 196, 219, 220 DAVID RUMSEY MAP COLLECTION
MAPS ON PAGES 193 & 194 LIBRARY OF CONGRESS COLLECTION

Recommended Reading about Lincoln, Gettysburg, and the Gettysburg Address
Michael Burlingame

The best one-volume account of the Gettysburg campaign is Allen C. Guelzo, <u>Gettysburg: The Last Invasion</u> (New York: Alfred A. Knopf, 2013), which supplants Edwin B. Coddington's, <u>The Gettysburg Campaign: A Study in Command</u> (New York: Scribner's, 1968), and Stephen W. Sears', <u>Gettysburg</u> (New York: Houghton Mifflin, 2003).

A useful companion volume of documentary selections is Rod Gragg, ed., <u>The Illustrated Gettysburg Reader: An Eyewitness History of the Civil War's Greatest Battle</u> (Washington: Regnery History, 2013), which contains an extensive, up-to-date bibliography.

Books about the Gettysburg Address are far less numerous than those about the campaign. The most thoughtful recent study is Martin P. Johnson's <u>Writing the Gettysburg Address</u> (Lawrence: University Press of Kansas, 2013). With Sherlock Holmes-like ingenuity and sophistication, the author solves a number of mysteries surrounding the composition, delivery, and reception of the speech. His strikingly original conclusions rest on exhaustive research and subtle analysis.

Gabor Boritt's <u>The Gettysburg Gospel: The Lincoln Speech That Nobody Knows</u> (New York: Simon & Schuster, 2006) explores at length the reception of the speech and traces its reputation over the decades since 1863.

Garry Wills won a Pulitzer Prize for <u>Lincoln at Gettysburg: The Words That Remade America</u> (New York: Simon & Schuster, 1992), which is especially useful in placing the Gettysburg cemetery in the context of nineteenth-century American cemetery design.

Although not specifically devoted to the Gettysburg Address, Douglas L. Wilson's <u>Lincoln's Sword: The Presidency and the Power of Words</u> (New York: Alfred A. Knopf, 2006) contains an insightful chapter on it.

Some older treatments of the speech that are still worth consulting include William E. Barton, <u>Lincoln at Gettysburg</u> (Indianapolis: Bobbs-Merrill, 1930); Louis A. Warren, <u>Lincoln's Gettysburg Declaration: "A New Birth of Freedom"</u> (Fort Wayne: Lincoln National Life Foundation, 1964); and Frank L. Klement, <u>The Gettysburg Soldiers' Cemetery and Lincoln's Address: Aspects and Angles</u> (Shippensburg, PA : White Mane, 1993).

About Our Underwriter

Our underwriter, John Warner IV, has a unique family heritage. He has two great-great-grandfathers and another great-grandfather, each having extraordinary careers, two having distinguished service in the Civil War, and each being friends with Illinois' leading citizen—Abraham Lincoln.

Clifton H. Moore, John Warner's paternal great-great-grandfather, was more than friends with Abraham Lincoln—the two were close associates practicing law for many years in Clinton, Illinois. Clifton H. Moore became the first resident attorney of DeWitt County in August, 1841. The town of Clinton, also the hometown of the Warner family, is the county seat.

Clinton was part of the Eighth Judicial Circuit when C. H. Moore met Abraham Lincoln, a lawyer who had begun regularly traveling "the circuit". Lincoln traveled the Eighth Judicial Circuit to Clinton, each spring and each fall for the semiannual court sessions. C. H. Moore had his law office along the town square (now John Warner's offices for Moore & Warner Farm Management), a short walk from the courthouse. Lincoln spent a great deal of time in Clifton Moore's office preparing cases and writing letters. Lincoln and Moore became close friends, and Lincoln would often visit and stay the night with the Moore family when traveling through Clinton. The Moore home where Lincoln stayed still stands on the east edge of town. A later home of C. H. Moore, an elegant Victorian mansion, is now the DeWitt County Museum. Called the C. H. Moore Homestead, the museum is a popular destination in the region and a centerpiece in the community.

Abraham Lincoln and C. H. Moore worked on many legal cases together, and opposed each other in many law cases also. Clifton Moore owned one of the largest private libraries in the state of Illinois outside of Chicago and Lincoln frequently spent time studying Moore's books. C. H. Moore was well-known for being a leading case law attorney, where Lincoln usually had a different approach in the courtroom.

Located at the town square, C. H. Moore's office was also near the center of community activities. In the 1840s and 1850s, it was here that Lincoln became equally well-known for fun and humorous activities.

John Warner maintains his great-great-grandfather Clifton H. Moore's office. Now home to Moore & Warner Farm Management, the office is a step into the past. While working on our last book, Abraham Lincoln Traveled This Way—The America Lincoln Knew, I discovered the building is a unique

Lincoln historical site and still operating as a business. The interior is preserved close to its original state, much like Lincoln would have seen it.

C. H. Moore attended the Republican National Convention of 1860 in Chicago, Lincoln staying in Springfield, as was the practice at that time. Moore worked with mutual close friend David Davis and others toward securing Lincoln's nomination for president. Although helping his friend Lincoln, Moore never had an interest in entering politics himself. He did form a land speculating partnership with Judge David Davis in 1848 that lasted until Judge Davis's death in 1886.

By the time the railroads came through Clinton in 1854, C. H. Moore had been a railroad attorney for the Illinois Central Railroad for over two years. The Illinois Central was the longest railroad in the world upon its completion in 1856. Lincoln often represented the railroad and although he lobbied for it, also had many cases against the Illinois Central.

Clifton Moore and Vespasian Warner, John Warner's great-grandfather, both passed on stories and anecdotes of Lincoln's numerous visits to Clinton and DeWitt County, recalling a number of cases that Lincoln prepared in C. H. Moore's office.

In one such case that came before the court of Judge David Davis, the Illinois Central Railroad was being sued by a farmer for damages ensuing from the construction of a right-of-way. Abraham Lincoln represented the Illinois Central and Lincoln's major political opponent, Stephen A. Douglas represented the farmer. The trial had to be postponed until the chief engineer of the Illinois Central, George B. McClellan, could come down from Chicago to testify. McClellan would later become Lincoln's top general of the Union Army during the early part of the Civil War. McClellan was frequently insubordinate and ineffective, and President Lincoln was forced to remove him.

John Warner's other great-great-grandfather was **Dr. John Warner**, the father of Vespasian Warner. He moved to DeWitt County in 1841 and practiced medicine for twelve years. A prominent citizen in Clinton, Dr. John Warner also knew Abraham Lincoln for many years. Because of Abraham Lincoln's routine visits twice a year, Lincoln became a good friend of Dr. Warner over the years.

At the first request for soldiers to protect the Union, Dr. Warner volunteered for military service in April, 1861, and helped organize the 41st Illinois Volunteer Infantry Regiment. Although he was a medical doctor,

HE CHOSE TO FIGHT AS A SOLDIER, MUSTERING IN AT THE RANK OF MAJOR. HE WAS IN THE BATTLES OF FORT HENRY, FORT DONELSON, AND SHILOH. THE 41ST ILLINOIS REGIMENT FOUGHT IN THE PEACH ORCHARD AT THE BATTLE OF SHILOH WHERE THE COMMANDER DIED IN BATTLE. WARNER THEN ASSUMED THE RANK OF LIEUTENANT COLONEL IN THE 41ST ILLINOIS REGIMENT. LATER IN THE WAR, COLONEL WARNER WAS FORCED TO RESIGN DUE TO ILLNESS AND RETURNED TO CLINTON.

WITH CONCERNS FOLLOWING THE WAR, DR. WARNER BECAME THE CHAIRMEN OF THE RELIEF OF WOUNDED SOLDIERS COMMITTEE IN CLINTON. HE SERVED AS A REPRESENTATIVE IN THE ILLINOIS LEGISLATURE. IN 1867, HE STARTED AN INVESTMENT HOUSE THAT WOULD LATER BECOME THE JOHN WARNER BANK. DR. WARNER ALSO PLANNED THE CONSTRUCTION OF A HOSPITAL IN CLINTON, WHICH HIS SON VESPASIAN WARNER COMPLETED.

JOHN WARNER'S GREAT-GRANDFATHER, **VESPASIAN WARNER**, ALSO KNEW ABRAHAM LINCOLN. AS A YOUNG MAN, HE MET LINCOLN WHEN THE EIGHTH JUDICIAL CIRCUIT WAS HOLDING THE SEMIANNUAL COURT SESSIONS IN CLINTON. LINCOLN CREATED A BIG IMPRESSION ON WARNER, WHO BEGAN TO STUDY LAW UNDER LAWRENCE WELDON, ANOTHER LINCOLN ASSOCIATE, WHEN THE CIVIL WAR BEGAN. VESPASIAN WARNER ENLISTED AND WAS MUSTERED INTO THE 20TH ILLINOIS VOLUNTEER INFANTRY REGIMENT AS A SERGEANT, AND LATER WAS PROMOTED TO CAPTAIN AND BREVET MAJOR. HE WAS IN THE BATTLES AT FORT HENRY, FORT DONELSON, SHILOH/PITTSBURG LANDING, VICKSBURG, AND ATLANTA.

AFTER SERVING IN THE INFANTRY, VESPASIAN WARNER SERVED ON THE STAFFS OF GENERALS SMITH, LEGGETT, AND LOGAN. HIS DUTY STARTED AS A QUARTERMASTER AND THEN LATER AS AN ORDNANCE OFFICER. WARNER WAS WOUNDED TWICE, FIRST A WOUND FROM A SWORD TO HIS FACE (WHICH LEFT A PERMANENT SCAR) AT THE BATTLE OF SHILOH. SECOND, HE HAD A HORSE SHOT OUT FROM UNDERNEATH HIM AT VICKSBURG AND THE HORSE FELL ON HIM. THIS RESULTED IN A PERMANENT INJURY, CAUSING HIM TO LIMP FOR THE REST OF HIS LIFE. AFTER THE CIVIL WAR, WARNER STAYED IN THE REGULAR ARMY, AND WAS SENT WEST TO ASSIST IN THE CONFLICT WITH HOSTILE INDIAN TRIBES. HE REACHED THE RANK OF MAJOR, BEFORE LEAVING THE ARMY IN JULY, 1866.

AFTER RETURNING FROM THE WEST, VESPASIAN WARNER WENT STRAIGHT TO HARVARD LAW SCHOOL, WHERE HE GRADUATED IN 1868. HE RETURNED TO CLINTON, AND MARRIED WINNIFRED MOORE, CLIFTON H. MOORE'S DAUGHTER. WARNER ENTERED A LAW PRACTICE WITH HIS FATHER-IN-LAW AND THE PARTNERSHIP DEVELOPED INTO MOORE & WARNER ATTORNEYS, LOCATED IN THE SAME OFFICES WHERE MOORE & WARNER FARM MANAGEMENT ARE PRESENTLY LOCATED.

VESPASIAN WARNER SERVED AS A REPUBLICAN CONGRESSMAN FOR TEN YEARS AND THEN ON MARCH 4, 1905, PRESIDENT THEODORE ROOSEVELT APPOINTED HIM COMMISSIONER OF PENSIONS. WARNER HELD THIS POSITION UNTIL NOVEMBER 25, 1909, AND WHILE COMMISSIONER, PASSIONATELY SERVED HIS FELLOW CIVIL WAR VETERANS.

A Day Long To Be Remembered—Lincoln in Gettysburg

Photography, concept, and book design by Robert Shaw
Written by Michael Burlingame
Captions by Robert Shaw
Primary Editing and Writing Consultation by Carol McFeeters Thompson
Editing by Tricia Shaw
Graphics by Robert and Tricia Shaw

Copyright © 2013 Firelight Publishing, an imprint of Wild Perceptions Publishing
All Photographs Copyright © Robert Shaw
Narrative Copyright © Michael Burlingame
Graphics Copyright © Robert and Tricia Shaw

All Rights Reserved
No photograph or portion of this book may be reproduced or transmitted in any form,
including electronically, without permission in writing from Firelight Publishing.
Abraham Lincoln handwriting typeface Copyright vLetter, Inc.

Requests for permission to make copies of any part of this book should be mailed to Firelight Publishing
at the address below.

All Abraham Lincoln writings and speeches in this book, referenced in Lincoln's handwriting, are part of
The Collected Works of Abraham Lincoln. Lincoln's words are presented true to the Collected Works—
quoted verbatim without indicating misspelled or missing words.

Paper produced, printed and bound 100% in the United States of America
Printed and bound by Walsworth Print Group, Marceline, Missouri
Printed on NewPage Sterling Premium dull 100lb. text #1
(contains 10% post-consumer recycled fiber content)

FSC® MIX Paper from responsible sources www.fsc.org FSC® C004755

For information about reproduction rights of the photographs in this book
and inquiries for purchasing photographic prints, please contact:

Firelight Publishing
Post Office Box 590
Heyworth, Illinois 61745
309.473.2994   10-4 p.m. ct, Monday-Friday
www.firelightpublishing.com
info@firelightpublishing.com

Also available from Firelight Publishing: Abraham Lincoln Traveled This Way — The America Lincoln Knew,
by Robert Shaw and Michael Burlingame, hardcover, 276 pages, published in 2011.

ISBN 978-1-891650-63-5
Library of Congress Control Number: 2013946839
First Edition

Dedication

Sergeant Royal J. Cooper of the 96th Illinois Infantry Regiment
Private David C. Radcliff of the 60th Illinois Infantry Regiment
Private Robert P. Manion of the 40th Illinois Infantry Regiment
Private Sidney D. Bagley of the 123rd Indiana Infantry Regiment
each of who fought for the Union in the Civil War.

Virgil Radcliffe and William Brown—
who gave the last full measure of devotion for their country in World War II.

Acknowledgements

To John Warner, IV, Michael Burlingame, and Carol McFeeters Thompson, I would like to give a **very sincere thanks** to each of you for your contribution and generous support. It was only through the friendship, dedication to this project, and professional integrity of each of you, that this book was possible. I consider myself very fortunate to be able to work with you and be associated with each of you.

To authors John Richter, Director of Imaging, and Bob Zeller, President, at The Center For Civil War Photography—your knowledge and assistance with the photographs from 1863 has been greatly appreciated. And to John, your detailed restoration work on the images for the book is absolutely amazing.

I also have a **very special thanks** to three ladies who are very supportive Lincoln admirers—Tricia Shaw, Miss Savannah Shaw, and Judy Shaw.

I want to thank my dear friends John Eden at the Long Nine Museum, Athens, and Wayne Temple, Lincoln scholar and author, for your research assistance and greatly appreciated encouragement.

I would also like to thank Rick Schubart; Kent Bangert, Moore & Warner Farm Managment; James Cornelius, Curator, Abraham Lincoln Presidential Library and Museum; Susan Haake, Curator and David Wachtveitl, Law Enforcement, Lincoln Home National Historic Site; Ann Tracy Mueller; Michelle Krowl, Civil War and Reconstruction Specialist, Manuscript Division, Library of Congress; Dan Ostendorf; David Rumsey, Cartography Associates; Garry Adelman, The Civil War Trust; Rick McKay, Lawrence Jackson and Chuck Kennedy at the White House Photo Office; Douglas L. Wilson; Dick and Joyce Manard; and Helen Stites.

In Gettysburg—special thanks to John Heiser, Historian, and Greg Goodell, Museum Services Supervisor, National Park Service, Gettysburg National Military Park; Mike and Stephanie Gladfelter; Jim and Susan Paddock; Benjamin K. Neely, Executive Director, Adams County Historical Society; David and Junko Young; George Lower and everyone at Lord Nelson's Gallery; Diane C.F. Brennan, Administrative Aide, Civil War Institute, the National Park Service, and the Gettysburg Presbyterian Church.

Thanks to the Abraham Lincoln Association for their outstanding work and for operating <u>The Collected Works of Abraham Lincoln</u> on-line database. We are indebted to Roy P. Basler, Editor, and staff, for compiling and creating the treasure <u>The Collected Works of Abraham Lincoln</u>.

Also thanks to the Papers of Abraham Lincoln for their ongoing work with The Lincoln Log: A Daily Chronology of the Life of Abraham Lincoln (a project of the Illinois Historic Preservation Agency and the Abraham Lincoln Presidential Library and Museum).

ROBERT SHAW HAS BEEN A PROFESSIONAL PHOTOGRAPHER FOR BOOKS AND CALENDARS FOR 27 YEARS. SHAW SPECIALIZES IN LANDSCAPE IMAGES, PHOTOGRAPHING THROUGHOUT THE UNITED STATES. HE IS THE CO-AUTHOR OF THE ACCLAIMED <u>ABRAHAM LINCOLN TRAVELED THIS WAY — THE AMERICA LINCOLN KNEW</u>, HIS FIRST COLLABORATION WITH MICHAEL BURLINGAME, PUBLISHED IN 2011. THE BOOK HAS BEEN WELL-RECEIVED FROM HISTORIANS TO YOUNG PEOPLE. ITS SUCCESS LED TO THE DEVELOPMENT OF <u>A DAY LONG TO BE REMEMBERED — LINCOLN IN GETTYSBURG</u>. A TWO-YEAR PROJECT, THIS BOOK IS UNIQUE AMONG BOOKS ON LINCOLN AND GETTYSBURG.

ROBERT SHAW IS A 1982 GRADUATE OF ILLINOIS STATE UNIVERSITY, WHERE HE BEGAN STUDYING PHOTOGRAPHY. FOLLOWING COLLEGE, SHAW STUDIED AT SEVERAL LEADING PHOTOGRAPHY PROGRAMS IN THE UNITED STATES. HE BEGAN WORKING AS A PHOTOGRAPHER PROFESSIONALLY IN 1986. SHAW WORKED WITH PUBLISHERS OF BOOKS, MAGAZINES, AND CALENDARS FOR TEN YEARS. IN 1997, HE STARTED WILD PERCEPTIONS PUBLISHING, AND LATER AN IMPRINT, FIRELIGHT PUBLISHING. SINCE 1997, WILD PERCEPTIONS PUBLISHING AND FIRELIGHT PUBLISHING HAVE SOLD OVER A MILLION COPIES OF BOOKS AND CALENDARS.

SHAW WORKED WITH LARGE & MEDIUM-FORMAT AND 35MM FILM CAMERAS FOR OVER 20 YEARS BEFORE MOVING TO DIGITAL CAMERAS IN 2005. MOST OF THE PHOTOGRAPHS IN HIS FIRST TWO BOOKS WERE MADE WITH 4x5 VIEW CAMERAS. ALL THE IMAGES IN <u>A DAY LONG TO BE REMEMBERED — LINCOLN IN GETTYSBURG</u> WERE MADE USING HIGH RESOLUTION DIGITAL CAMERAS. ALONG WITH THE PHOTOGRAPHY & DIGITAL DARKROOM, SHAW DOES THE PROJECT RESEARCH, CONCEPT AND LAYOUT, GRAPHIC DESIGN, AND OVERSEES THE FOUR-COLOR PRINTING & BINDING FOR ALL HIS BOOKS AND CALENDARS.

ROBERT SHAW'S PHOTOGRAPHY FROM ACROSS THE UNITED STATES HAS BEEN WIDELY DISPLAYED IN HOMES, BUSINESSES, MUSEUMS, UNIVERSITIES, AND OTHER NON-PROFIT ORGANIZATIONS. HIS IMAGES HAVE APPEARED ON THE COVERS AND INSIDE MANY MAGAZINES, BOOKS, AND CALENDARS. SHAW'S OTHER BOOKS INCLUDE <u>ILLINOIS — SEASONS OF LIGHT</u>, CACHE RIVER PRESS (1997) AND <u>WINDY CITY WILD — CHICAGO'S NATURAL WONDERS</u>, CHICAGO REVIEW PRESS (1999). HIS PHOTOGRAPHY HAS ALSO BEEN PUBLISHED IN BOOKS BY ABRAMS BOOKS AND NATIONAL GEOGRAPHIC BOOKS. SHAW'S IMAGES FROM GETTYSBURG AND LINCOLN SITES HAVE BEEN USED BY THE ABRAHAM LINCOLN PRESIDENTIAL LIBRARY & MUSEUM, THE UNIVERSITY OF ILLINOIS, THE OLD STATE CAPITOL FOUNDATION, THE LOOKING FOR LINCOLN HERITAGE COALITION, THE ILLINOIS HISTORIC PRESERVATION AGENCY, AND THE ILLINOIS DEPT. OF COMMERCE AND COMMUNITY AFFAIRS. ROBERT SHAW'S PHOTOGRAPHY HAS BEEN FEATURED ON THE COVERS AND INSIDE <u>FOUR SCORE AND SEVEN</u> (ABRAHAM LINCOLN PRESIDENTIAL LIBRARY & MUSEUM QUARTERLY MAGAZINE) AND ILLINOIS HERITAGE (A PUBLICATION OF THE ILLINOIS STATE HISTORICAL SOCIETY).

Michael Burlingame is a renowned Lincoln scholar and Civil War historian. His biography <u>Abraham Lincoln: A Life</u>, two volumes published by Johns Hopkins University Press (2008), is the preeminent biography in the study of Lincoln. He is the writer of the acclaimed <u>Abraham Lincoln Traveled This Way — The America Lincoln Knew</u>, the first collaboration with Robert Shaw, published in 2011. He is also the author of <u>Lincoln and the Civil War</u> (2011) and <u>The Inner World of Abraham Lincoln</u>, published by the University of Illinois Press (1994). He has edited a dozen books of Lincoln primary source materials: <u>An Oral History of Abraham Lincoln: John G. Nicolay's Interviews and Essays</u>; <u>Inside Lincoln's White House: The Complete Civil War Diary of John Hay</u>; <u>Lincoln Observed: Civil War Dispatches of Noah Brooks</u>; <u>Lincoln's Journalist: John Hay's Anonymous Writings for the Press, 1860-1864</u>; <u>A Reporter's Lincoln by Walter B. Stevens</u>; <u>With Lincoln in the White House: Letters, Memoranda, and Other Writings of John G. Nicolay, 1860-1865</u>; <u>At Lincoln's Side: John Hay's Civil War Correspondence and Selected Writings</u>; <u>Inside the White House in War Times: Memoirs and Reports of Lincoln's Secretary by William O. Stoddard</u>; <u>Dispatches from Lincoln's White House: The Anonymous Civil War Journalism of Presidential Secretary William O. Stoddard</u>; <u>The Real Lincoln: A Portrait by Jesse W. Weik</u>; <u>"Lincoln's Humor" and Other Essays by Benjamin P. Thomas</u>; and <u>Abraham Lincoln: The Observations of John G. Nicolay and John Hay</u>.

Professor Burlingame received his B.A. from Princeton University and his Ph.D. from Johns Hopkins University. In 1968 he joined the History Department at Connecticut College, where he taught until 2001 as the May Buckley Sadowski Professor of History Emeritus. He joined the faculty of the University of Illinois at Springfield in 2009. Professor Burlingame has received numerous awards and honors for his scholarly research and writing. He received the Abraham Lincoln Association Book Prize in 1996, the Lincoln Diploma of Honor from Lincoln Memorial University in 1998, Honorable Mention for the Lincoln Prize, Gettysburg College in 2001, and was inducted into the Lincoln Academy of Illinois in 2009. Professor Burlingame is presently the holder of the Chancellor Naomi B. Lynn Distinguished Chair in Lincoln Studies at UIS.

The masterfully researched and written biography <u>Abraham Lincoln: A Life</u> won the 2010 Lincoln Prize, sponsored by the Gilder-Lehrman Institute for American History and Gettysburg College, for the finest scholarly work in English on Abraham Lincoln, or the American Civil War soldier, or a subject relating to their era. It also was a co-winner of the annual book prize awarded by the Abraham Lincoln Institute of Washington, D.C., and won the Russell P. Strange Book Award given annually by the Illinois State Historical Society for the best book on Illinois history.

UNION ARTILLERY POSITION ON EAST CEMETERY HILL WITH CULP'S HILL IN THE DISTANCE, BELOW THE RISING SUN.
THE CANNON IN THE FOREGROUND IS BETWEEN 250 AND 280 YARDS FROM WHERE
ABRAHAM LINCOLN DELIVERED THE MOST FAMOUS 272 WORDS IN HISTORY.

PAGES 216 & 217: HEAVY FIGHTING RAGED AROUND EVERY SIDE OF DEVIL'S DEN. UNION POSITIONS FIRST OCCUPIED THE
MAZE OF BOULDERS. IT WAS CAPTURED BY THE CONFEDERATES ON JULY 2, THEN REGAINED BY FEDERAL TROOPS AFTER THE RETREAT.